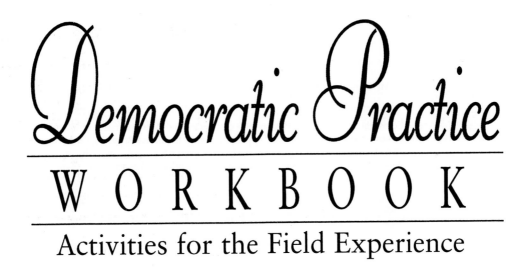

Democratic Practice
WORKBOOK
Activities for the Field Experience

Caroline R. Pryor
Northern Arizona University

Forewords by

Joel Spring
State University of New York at New Paltz

Gary G. Bitter
Arizona State University

McGraw Hill

Boston   Burr Ridge, IL   Dubuque, IA   Madison, WI   New York   San Francisco   St. Louis
Bangkok   Bogotá   Caracas   Lisbon   London   Madrid
Mexico City   Milan   New Delhi   Seoul   Singapore   Sydney   Taipei   Toronto

McGraw-Hill Higher Education

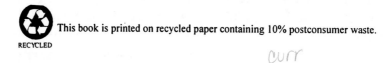

A Division of The McGraw·Hill Companies

DEMOCRATIC PRACTICE WORKBOOK: ACTIVITIES FOR THE FIELD EXPERIENCE

This book is printed on recycled paper containing 10% postconsumer waste.

RECYCLED

2 3 4 5 6 7 8 9 0 QPD/QPD 0 9

Gift 4/00

curr
H
625
.U5
P79
2000

ISBN 0-07-232568-2

Editorial director: *Jane E. Vaicunas*
Sponsoring editor: *Beth Kaufman*
Editorial coordinator: *Teresa Wise*
Senior marketing manager: *Daniel M. Loch*
Project manager: *Joyce M. Berendes*
Senior production supervisor: *Sandra Hahn*
Designer: *K. Wayne Harms*
Typeface: *10/12 Times Roman*
Printer: *Quebecor Printing Book Group/Dubuque, IA*

Cover designer: *Jamie O'Neal*
Cover photograph: *PhotoDisc 41 education 2*

Preface

Democratic Practice Workbook: Activities for the Field Experience was written to help students at various levels of their field experience to observe their mentor teachers and begin to participate in the classroom. It is a guide with forms for reflecting on these experiences. The forms contain focused questions so that the observer/participant can define and make sense of democratic classroom practice.

This workbook may also be helpful to graduate students who have had some teaching experience and are now extending their education. These teachers are often trying new methods of curriculum design and are re-thinking former approaches to their teaching.

Finally, the workbook may be used as a focus of a social studies methods course and a means to identify explicit methods desired in a content that requires reflection on American citizenship.

The book is organized around three main themes of democracy: Liberty and Freedom (**LF**), Justice and Fairness (**JF**), and Equality and Equal Opportunity (**EEO**). All of the observation forms ask the student to observe for these themes in the classroom or school and to report their findings on forms related to various classroom activities such as textbook selection or grading procedures.

Each form contains focus questions that are central to pedagogical issues as well as emphasizing the subject content area. The forms are intended for in-depth reflection with discourse between students and mentor-teachers at their schools and with the university professor in their courses.

Organization of the Text

Part One of the text is an overview of the role of schooling and citizenship in America and identifies the text's three main themes of **LF**, **JF**, and **EEO**.
A full discussion of these themes and their historical roots is found in Appendix B. Part One also includes a *To the Instructor* section that offers tips for guiding student observations and a sample topic guide for three semesters of field observation.

Part Two contains the Observation/Participation Guide and Forms.
Chapter One describes what students can expect at their school sites complete with student tips on how to use the observation forms. Sample completed observation forms are provided to help students begin filling in their forms.
Chapter Two presents the Democratic Discourse Model of Observation.
Chapter Three introduces observation of classroom instruction and contains forms for observing in the classroom. Each topic discussed includes a strategy section that students can use as a focus during their observations or when they participate in teaching. Each observation form also includes a section for reflection on democratic practice.

Chapter Four helps students begin to participate in the classroom with a guide on how to write comprehensive lesson plans. The three elements of democracy, **LF, JF, EEO,** are again a theme in this discussion, and the themes appear on the lesson planning forms. The plans also include a section for student/mentor reflection on the lesson.

Part Three provides an opportunity for students, mentors, and professors to discuss and analyze democratic classroom practice.

Chapter One is a guided section with tips for locating and analyzing democratic concepts on their observation forms.

Chapter Two discusses the roles and goals of schools and society and includes a review of notions of citizenship and historical concepts, and it introduces the utility of the National Professional Teaching Standards Board (emphasis—History/Social Studies Standards).

Chapter Three continues the students' practice in reflecting on **LF, JF,** and **EEO** in democratic practice and contains sample case studies with reflection scenarios, extended questions, suggested curriculum projects, and sample classroom activities.

Chapter Four is a guide for writing a philosophy of education statement. Four orientations to teaching are identified, and two writing methods are fully listed. Students are shown how to use either a chunking method or a belief method of writing, and the focus is on writing a statement of democratic educational beliefs.

Chapter Five is a summary statement of the importance of democratic practice to education and student attainment. A call for creating International Standards of Democratic Practice is included in this chapter.

Appendices

Appendix A contains an observation form for the National Professional Teaching Standards Board-History/Social Studies Standards.

Appendix B provides definitions of liberty/freedom, justice/fairness, and equality/equal opportunity and a lengthy discussion of the historical roots of these themes.

Appendix C presents qualitative tables of relevant individuals in history and the main themes of their philosophies.

Appendix D describes three curriculum models: Tyler, Taba, and Oliva.

Acknowledgments

Developing Democratic Practice: Activities for the Field Experience is a product of having spent over ten years as a university supervisor observing student teachers in their field experience. In conversation held often in lunchrooms as well as in classrooms, the students reflect on, debate, and critique new ways to teach, consistently reflecting on what they've learned at the university during former field experiences such as internships and volunteer work. In one case, I was observing a student teacher in a secondary school site, while two intern/observers were also watching this student. I asked the two observers what they noticed in the lesson and they replied, "I don't know." My guess is that they were watching the overall effect of the student teacher on her interaction with the class, but they were not certain exactly which practices were important to note.

Given this information, I asked if they had some special interest in the practice of teaching (i.e., what they were looking for). Again, the two observers were unsure of how to focus their observations and, once focused, were unsure of how to describe their insights in written form for their professors. Thus, I began thinking of a tool to support their field experience. In so doing, I read and re-read some of my own recent publications, those involving the American experience with democracy.

Finally, I asked myself what in the experience of American teachers could be defined and termed *democratic in practice*. And, indeed, could experienced and novice teachers, interns, and student teachers identify these practices for themselves and for their mentees? If as a profession we could determine a set of values that cuts across all curricula, all types of schools, and find a sense of common understandings about democracy, could we share these insights as practices with our next generation of teachers, the intern and student teachers in the field experience?

This is a text about how America implements teaching practices that support critical values of a democracy: liberty and individual freedom, justice and fairness, and equality and equal opportunity. It also is a text for America's universities, as it is in just such an education that practice and the practitioner's eye is formed and reinforced. Let us hope that Thomas Jefferson's invocation to us all that every citizen should be well educated continues as we begin with certainty and dedication to our teachers!

I have been fortunate to work with and learn from many scholars in areas that support the field experience, mentor-teachers and their students among them. I have also had the immeasurable good fortune to be mentored and at times challenged to create a text that examines democratic practice in a manner that appears both historical and practical for the classroom.

I am grateful to have worked with and learned from Thomas McGowan, Nicholas Appleton, Don Freeman and Gloria Smith at Arizona State University, and Jim Davis and Janet Quade of Northern Arizona University. Their insight and support have been invaluable.

I am further grateful to the members of the Commission on Democratic Practices of the Association of Teacher Educators who have taken the time and energy to complete a needs assessment for the text and suggest additions to the text: Art Pearl and Kay Terry, co-chairs, and Paul Joseph Barnes, Paul Black, John Bucci, Armando Laguardia, Fred Curtis, Jerry Ligon, Joseph Macaluso, and Mary Williams.

Scholarship and critique of teaching would never have entered my world without the wisdom, support, and friendship of my former doctoral chair, Nelson L. Haggerson, Professor Emeritus, and Fulbright Scholar, Arizona State University. Nelson's embodiment of justice and fairness, evidenced always in his publications and administrative practice, reinforce to me everyday that one never journeys alone.

The scholarly contributions of Gary G. Bitter and Brandt W. Pryor, Arizona State University, and Joel Spring, State University of New York, College at New Paltz, are gratefully acknowledged and very much appreciated. They again remind me that scholarship is collaboration at its best.

The hard work and detailed contributions of the reviewers of *Democratic Practice Workbook* has been extraordinary! I so appreciate their attention to theoretical perceptions and their help in fine-tuning the text's organization. My sincere thanks to: John Bucci, Rhode Island College; Jaylynne N. Hutchinson, Ohio University; Arthur Newman, University of Florida; Mary John O'Hair, University of Oklahoma; Julie Rainer, Georgia State University; Tony Sanchez, Purdue University; Kay W. Terry, Western Kentucky University; and Mary Williams, University of San Diego. You are terrific!

No scholarly work sees the light of publication without the vision and support of a fine editor. I sincerely thank Beth Kaufman, Senior Editor, McGraw-Hill. She believed in, encouraged, and supported this text. McGraw-Hill's extraordinary editing support team, Terri Wise and Joyce Berendes' efforts are very much appreciated. Thank you both for your talent and time in working on this project. I also would like to thank John Dahlberg for his diligent efforts in editing and formatting the text.

Finally, with fortune at my side, I wish to thank Brandt Pryor, Senior Research Scientist at Arizona State University's Technology Based Learning and Research. His scholarship and breadth of experience in reading about history has been a model for which we all can re-set both our moral compass and our intellectual goal: *read so you will know!*

Foreword

Foreword by Joel Spring

Issued during the United Nations' Decade for Human Rights Education, Caroline Pryor's *Democratic Classroom Practice: Activities for the Field Experience* fulfills the international pledge to help student teachers and teachers to understand the meaning of democracy in the classroom. Democratic practices are an important part of the worldwide effort at human rights education. The 1993 Vienna World Conference on Human Rights proclaimed that teaching about democratic traditions was an essential part of human rights education. This action made instruction in democratic practices an essential part of the right to education guaranteed by the 1948 Universal Declaration of Human Rights. Officially issued on July 12, 1993, Article 79 of the Vienna Declaration & Programme of Action "calls on all States to include human rights, humanitarian law, democracy, and rule of law as subjects in the curricula of all learning institutions in formal and non-formal setting. "In Article 80, the document states that "Human rights education should include peace, democracy, development and social justice as set forth in international and regional human rights instruments." In March 1995, the General Assembly issued its official resolution declaring the United Nations' Decade for Human Rights Education. The resolution advocates a human rights education that provides more than information about the rights protected by international covenants and declarations. The resolution states that human rights education "should constitute a comprehensive life-long process by which people at all levels in development and in all strata of society learn respect for the dignity of others and the means and methods of ensuring that respect in all societies." Consequently, the resolution asserts that human rights education should include attitudinal (dignity of others) and activist (ensuring the respect in all societies) objectives. Professor Pryor's workbook provides the classroom observer with guidelines for understanding the attitudinal and activist aspects of democratic traditions. Using this workbook, observers can identify and evaluate democratic classroom practices. After reflecting on their observations, students will understand how their actions as teachers can reflect democratic principles. As far as I know, this is the only workbook that meets the requirements of the right to education in human rights and that will help teachers understand how they can fulfill their commitment to democracy and human rights.

Joel Spring
State University of New York
College at New Paltz

Foreword by Gary G. Bitter

For at least four decades, science fiction writers and philosophers have warned us about the dramatic changes that computers will make in our lives. As we near the year 2000, we find that computers are so pervasive in our lives that such warnings are no longer academic. Although many, if not most, purposes for which computers are used are extremely beneficial to the individual and to society, there are a number of negative aspects to computer use.

Current research in technology-based education seems to offer more questions than answers about the potentially negative effects of computer use on society. Research has demonstrated at least two problems that most concern me, as a technology educator and as a citizen, and that I believe poses problems for a democratic and just society.

The first, and I believe most difficult, problem is the currently inequitable distribution of computer use, by socioeconomic status and by gender. Left unresolved, this problem will result in a relatively small technological elite and a large technologically deprived proletariat. On its face, this is a clear threat to a democratic society. This technological elite will have disproportionately greater access to the best jobs, with higher salaries, better fringe benefits, and a generally superior lifestyle. Those who are technologically deprived will be severely disadvantaged, not only in employment but also in limited access to information, entertainment, and much else.

This concern about equity in computer access has two parts: socioeconomic status and gender. Affluent school districts have many—and up-to-date—computers available to their students and can afford to hire highly skilled computer education specialists to help students and teachers use computers effectively. Low-income districts, on the other hand, tend to have many fewer—and much older—computers and typically rely for computer use assistance on teachers who are not professionally trained in that field. Grants from government at many levels, and from business and industry, have begun to address this gap in computer access, but much more needs to be done.

The second aspect to inequity in computer access is the "gender gap" between boys and girls. Boys appear to naturally gravitate toward computers; they are both more interested and more involved with technology than are girls. This gap has been documented, but not fully explained, by research. Part of the problem might be the design of software, which generally tends to emphasize male-dominated activities. Games often include violence and competition as motivators.

The second major problem that computers pose for a democratic and just society is the entirely new range of possibilities for unethical behavior presented by technology. Such unethical uses of computers include theft of computer time, theft of software (piracy), and plagiarism (e.g., term papers downloaded from the Internet).

These issues present new dilemmas for practicing classroom teachers. What can teachers do to counteract these negative influences of technology? Regarding equity issues, teachers must strive to provide equal access to computers for all students, regardless of socioeconomic status or gender. Grant programs—some of which are designed for teacher-initiated proposals—can ease the problem of financial limitations. Teachers must also take care in the selection of software, to ensure that programs that will appeal to girls are included in the classroom. Regarding ethical issues, the most powerful lesson teachers provide is their own ethical use of computers. Without this positive example, anything else they do is likely to be for naught. In addition, teachers can use simulations or have students role-play situations concerning ethical problems with computer use. These techniques, along with frank discussion of the issues, will lay the groundwork for students' ethical use of computers.

Fortunately, teachers have at their disposal some useful tools to help them with these new problems. The first is a set of standards prepared by the International Society for Technology in Education (ISTE), which deals with many of these issues. See www.iste.org for further information. The second useful tool that teachers have is this new book of Caroline Pryor's, which will help them observe in the classroom and identify elements of democratic practice.

Gary G. Bitter, Ph.D.
Professor and Chair, Educational Media and Computers Graduate Program and Director, Technology Based Learning and Research, Arizona State University, Tempe, AZ

Contents

PART ONE 1

THE ROLE OF SCHOOLING AND CITIZENSHIP IN AMERICA 1
   The Role of Discourse in Democracy 1
   A Citizen's Educational Preparation for Participation in Society 2
   Addressing Issues of Power and Authority 3
   Community as a Foundation for Democracy: Negotiation, Consensus, and Majority Rules .. 4
WHAT ARE OUR NATIONAL GOALS? 6
   Standards for Teaching Social Studies—History 7
   A Few Words about Schools and Practice 9
TO THE INSTRUCTOR 11
   Sample Semester Observation Format 14
   Using the Observation Forms 16
   Tips for the Instructor 17

PART TWO: A GUIDE TO OBSERVING AND PARTICIPATING IN SCHOOLS 18

CHAPTER ONE
   What to Expect at Elementary, Middle, and Secondary School Sites 19
      Elementary Schools 19
      Middle Schools 21
      Secondary Schools 22
      Using the Observation Guide 23
      Forms for Data Collection 28
CHAPTER TWO
   Observing with a Model for Democratic Discourse 32
      Democratic Discourse Model 32
      Questions to Guide the Use of the Model 33
      How to Use the Discourse Model for Democratic Practice 33
      Selecting a Democratic Practice Focus 34
      Discourse Model for Democratic Practice 37
CHAPTER THREE
   Types of Classroom Instruction 39
      The Classroom Environment 51
      Supplies and Resources 54
      Classroom Management 55
      Classroom Environment Observation Form 60
      Observation of Classroom Management Form 61
      Technology and Other Applied Projects 66
      Observation of Worksheets Form 70
      Observation of Books Form 71
      Observation of Tests Form 72
      Observation of Reports and Text Material Form 73
      Observation of Books for Civics Education Form 74

Observation of Technology Use Form 75
Observation of Multi-Media, Tapes, Video and Photos.. 76
Observation of Homework and Projects Due Form 77
Evaluation and Grading... 78
Observation of Grading on a Bell Curve or a Percentage Grading Scale Form 85
Observation of Creativity, Effort/Improvement, and Resources in Evaluation 86
Observation of Portfolio Evaluation Form 87
Observation of Age/Grade and Content Alignment Form.. 88
Observation of Narrative Evaluation Form 89
Observation of Extra-Credit/Mastery Model Form 90
Special Education 91
Gifted Programs.. 92
Language Acquisition Programs 93
Technology and Computers 95
Media Labs and Libraries 98
Music, Art, and Physical Education 99
Observation of Special Education and Gifted Form.. 104
Observation of Language Acquisition Form 105
Observation of Technology, Computers, and Software Form................................... 106
Observation of Technology, Computers, and Software Form................................... 107
Observation of Counselors: Academic, Career, and Special Needs Form 108
Observation of Music, Art, and Physical Education Form.. 109
Adjunct Activities... 110
Observation of School Rules: Character and Civic Behavior Form......................... 115
Observation of Special Events (Sports, Teams, and Plays) Form 116
District Policies, Government, and the Law... 117
Observation of District Policies Form 120
Observation of Government and the Law Form 121
Community and Business Participation.. 122
Observation of Parent Volunteers, Booster and Parent Clubs, and Business Partnerships.. 124

CHAPTER FOUR
Preparing to Participate in Classrooms 125
Planning to Participate! 125
Writing a Lesson Plan... 126
Instructional Steps to the Lesson 129
Closure in a Lesson Plan 131
Resources for Lesson Plans 132
Reflecting on Your Lesson Plan 134
Form for Writing Lesson Plans 136

PART THREE: WHAT IS DEMOCRATIC PRACTICE IN SCHOOLS? 137

CHAPTER ONE
Making Sense of Democratic Practice.. 138
Locating and Analyzing Democratic Concepts in Your Observation Form 138
Reflecting on Democratic Practice 139
National Standards for Teaching Social Studies—History 140
Application of the Model of Democratic Discourse Form 142
Application of the National Standards for Teaching Social Studies—History Form 143

Organizing Data/Identifying Themes of Democracy Form.................................144

CHAPTER TWO

Building the Future of Democracy 145
Reflecting on the Roles and Goals of Schools and Society..........................145
Building an Individual Philosophy of Democratic Education..........................146
Responsibilities of Citizenship 148
National Board for Professional Teaching Standards—Teaching Social Studies—History 150

CHAPTER THREE

Applications of the Roots of Democracy...151
Applied Project..156
Students' Role in Questioning..159
Applied Project..162
Example Curriculum Project 165
Examples of Classroom Practice 166
Applied Project..167

CHAPTER FOUR

Writing a Philosophy Statement of Democratic Educational Beliefs 168
Writing a Statement of Practices and Beliefs...170

CHAPTER FIVE

Summary 172
A Call for International Standards of Democratic Practice..............................173

APPENDICES...176

Appendix A: National Board for Professional Teaching Standards—Social Studies-History...177
Appendix B: Historical Roots and Definitions...180
Appendix C: Qualitative Tables...187
Appendix D: Curriculum Models 190
ABOUT THE AUTHOR..193

REFERENCES...194

Part One

The Role of Schooling and Citizenship in America

… democracy is a form of political governance involving the consent of the governed and equality of opportunity.

(Apple, 1995, p. 6)

The Role of Discourse in Democracy

Talk, talk, talk! Radio blasts! News reports on TV! Newspaper and magazine grinds! Best seller lists and audiotapes. Campaign signs along a roadway. Advertising on a carton of milk.

Is it noise? Or is it discourse? Does freedom reign? Or are rules supreme?

Who makes these rules? Do I like them? Can I say so? What happens if I cannot?

I wonder what teachers tell kids about democracy. I wonder what messages they already have formed.

Are we free? Do we care about one another? Can we all achieve our goals?

> Sure, we are free.
> We have an ethos of fairness.
> I can grow up to be president of the United States.

One doesn't have to look far to discern patterns in the way Americans speak to one another. Our days are filled with TV talk news reports regarding events of the day and inferences about why the events occurred. Discourse (conversation), it appears, has great appeal in the American focus of higher-order thinking and concomitant inquiry. Americans are practiced in this cultural norm, *using strategies of discourse.* Both smooth talkers and the well spoken have idealized a set of values (e.g., we have faith in our ability to tell others what we think).

Historically, we have always been a nation of conversationalists. We have to look no further than the First Amendment to the United States Constitution to support how we value free speech:

Amendment I (1791)

Congress shall make no law respecting an establishment of religion or prohibiting the free exercise thereof; or abridging the freedom of speech, or of the press; or the right of the people to peaceably assemble, and to petition the government for a redress of grievances.

(Ravitch, 1992)

Individual philosophy or approach to one's role in society (e.g., a teacher's role) can influence expectations of how we converse with one another. For example, Jonas Soltis (Fenstermacher and Soltis, 1992) writes about a philosophical approach to teaching termed *the interpretivist approach* as he explains that communication, not just speech, is an implicit part of sending and receiving messages.

Two notions about communication or discourse should help explain how we can define the attributes of a democratic nation. First, freedom to converse allows each person to express his/her own ideas, and, second, discourse about ideas allows each individual to first hear and then choose the ideas he/she prefers. Thus, in a free society, independence of expression leads to independence or freedom in thought and in life.

A Citizen's Educational Preparation for Participation in Society

Knowing that we have the right to converse freely is not the same as knowing *how* to converse well. Models of discourse can be taught, and teachers with insight into democratic practice can use these models to further a student's skill in both speech and inquiry. The basis for preparation for participation in a democratic society, vis-à-vis an educated citizenry, has been highly regarded by several of our founding fathers, Benjamin Franklin and Thomas Jefferson among them.

The caveat to be well educated is expressed by Jefferson in redressing the potential for tyranny in societies without such a well-educated populace. He writes (in 1779), in a section titled *A Bill for the More General Diffusion of Knowledge*, a purposeful piece warning governments that those entrusted with power could, in effect, succumb to personal ambition and defeat the natural purpose of a free society. This purpose should be the promotion of public happiness (Foner, 1944). Interestingly, Jefferson refers to the gatekeepers of happiness as those rendered with "the sacred deposition of the rights and liberties of their fellow citizen…those who are 'fully fit' to prevent degeneracy in a free government" (p. 40).

It appears that our forefathers were dedicated to the creation of a government that could be "administered well" (Ravitch, 1992). Benjamin Franklin, speaking to the attendees at the Constitutional Convention of 1787, reminded his audience that, while he had no expectation of perfection in a social document such as a constitution, he proposed that we do have the use of "joint wisdom" and could by nature sacrifice to the public good. Franklin expected an imperfect document to be executed perfectly due to the "wisdom and integrity of its governors' (1992, p. 111).

Addressing Issues of Power and Authority

Relying on the Constitution to safeguard freedom of speech is not the same thing as defining issues of who speaks and what power they have when they do speak. For example, the Constitution is a document written as a framework for democracy, often non-prescriptive in addressing areas such as personal practices and activities. Most citizens (and teachers), therefore, are left to interpret the Constitution and in effect become one of a child's first formal models of power and authority.

In writing about the influence that schools exert over the mind of a child, Joel Spring in his 1998 text, *Wheels in the Head,* writes, "Most government schools are coercive institutions" (p. 15). Schools represent a powerful authority in the way students think; coercion, it appears, may be a directive that is owed in part to teacher practices (Soltis, 1992; Wactler, 1997).

Teachers have had a history of individual freedom in organizing their classroom practice. While Spring (1998) writes that "whenever a government runs a school system, they might try to perpetuate their power by influencing the knowledge and attitudes disseminated by the school system" (p. 15), it is unlikely that any government can entirely diminish the values and beliefs of an individual teacher.

We draw on notions of individual power from precedents established by writers such as John Stuart Mill (1806-1873). Can a democracy address issues of fairness in authority and power? Where should authority (particularly authority of the classroom teacher) lie? Should the teacher remain as the objective or domineering force correct in his/her perception of his/her classroom role?

Mill, in his most famous treatise, *On Liberty* (Gutmann, 1996; Ravitch, 1992), asserts that freedom of individual right and opinion predominates over government goals.

Let's ask ourselves to reflect on the role of the teacher:

Should teachers decide on practice in their classrooms? Amy Gutmann (1996, p. 224), citing Robson, writes that the following Millian principle could be a starting point for just such a debate:

Over himself, over his own body and mind, the individual is sovereign.
(John Stuart Mill in Robson, 1977)

I wonder if teachers feel that they have this control, and I wonder if they teach this spirit of free thought to their students. If they build a foundation for professional authority, what practices and activities do they use? I wonder, asks the teacher.

> "Can I or should I negotiate with students?"
> "Should I have students vote on classroom rules?"
> "Is it fair to say that the majority rules?"
> "What will I tell them about democracy?"

Community as a Foundation for Democracy: Negotiation, Consensus, and Majority Rules

How do schools create an environment that "feels fair"? In other words, should schools negotiate with students and community to become actively engaged as partners in decision making? Derived from notions of a participatory and conscientious voice, John Locke in a retrospective and prescriptive entree to how society should treat and create a civil society, wrote (in *The Second Treatise of Civil Government*, 1690) that negotiation for civil concerns (as in a concern for the commonwealth or community) necessitates a giving up of one's freedom (Ravitch, 1992). Consensus in community occurs, Locke offers, because it is the only way a *civil society can be defined* (p. 39). By this definition, the giving up of one's freedom in order to consent to and align with the needs of the body politic is all that is required for the true execution of free will.

It appears, then, that the first order of discourse is with self. The first step is to negotiate classroom issues with oneself. Teachers could reflect on questions such as What are my goals? and What do I see as my personal role (as the teacher)?

A teacher further collaborates with the community to build a consensus of options of school goals. Through this interaction, the community then authorizes the government (vis-à-vis public schools) to govern for the good of one people. The community trusts that its voice will be heard and that its natural right to freedom will not be quashed.

Controversial issues occur, issues such as requiring students to wear uniforms in public schools or placing special needs children in mainstream classrooms. The negotiation treads heavily when representing every voice.

Perhaps we could respond by stating that if the majority of a community believes in school uniforms then uniforms should be required. Can there be room for negotiation when every voice does not agree? Should every voice have to agree to create a civil society?

Perhaps we should turn first to how we represent the minority voice. Zuchert (1991) wrote that de Tocqueville insisted on the paradigm of critical thought to disengage or disempower that status quo (of majority rules) (p. 143). The apparent concern was that the minority voice would find it "difficult to find allies to resist it [the majority]" (p. 142) and further implement a leveling oppression in the process of negotiation. Evidence Zuchert's report of de Tocqueville's understanding of the order of power in a democracy:

> *Is it possible to conceive a people without castes, hierarchy, or classes, in which the law, recognizing no privileges, divisions in inheritances equally and which at the same time, has neither culture nor freedom?*
>
> (Zuchert, 1991, p. 143)

Where, then, could the minority voice turn in negotiation for social consensus? Tocqueville wrote a sincere tribute to America, marked in his mind by a uniqueness of conditions (for community building) and negotiation in good faith (a habit he greatly admired):

> *The mind became an element in success; knowledge became a tool of government and intellect a social force, and educated men played a part in affairs of state.*
>
> (Tocqueville, 1838, p. 40)

Apparently, de Tocqueville had great confidence in the American implementation of consistency in the social values of freedom and equality, and he satisfied this faith by regarding consensus as a natural outcome and assumed therefore that liberty was the natural state of humainty (Schleifer, 1991).

Teachers could negotiate in good faith with community members, and within their classroom. In an era of enlightenment, human nature would prevail upon the majority to integrate minority views in a democratic debate about approaches to teaching.

A clear examination of democratic practice democratic practices, activities and strategies might reveal that the negotiation for equality is less than the envisioned foundation for community. Teachers and educational leaders might want to re-acquaint themselves with the subtleties of the central doctrines of democracy: **Liberty and individual freedom, justice and fairness**, and **equality and equal opportunity** (Wactler, 1997b, 1999).

What Are Our National Goals?

When considering how to create democratic practice in our schools, we have to consider the community in which our schools are placed. For example, when students write about community values, one prized purpose appears to be the goals of the community itself. In other words, it may be that it is the "common good that is a central feature of democracy" (Apple, 1995, p. 11).

It *may* be that the common good looms larger in American culture than the core value of individuality or freedom. Or it may be that, without equal opportunity, neither the value of the good of the whole nor fairness is available to many within the community.

How then can we create a sense of National Goals when even within our own communities we are unsure of the balance between common good and individual rights? Finally, how do we ever know what is fair and what is just?

Perhaps we should look to a common set of goals for our citizens. National Goals (or core values), then, can be emphasized as important to a democratic society. Argument for such a set of goals can be found in the writing of authors such as Amy Gutmann, who writes that democracy must be overtly taught (1999), or Apple and Beane (1995), who write that the conditions of reform from inequality must be experienced in schools to make a lasting difference in the eventual lives of children, educators, and communities served by the schools.

Consider the following as a set of National Goals for democratic schools:

> ➤ Each student should **demonstrate** democratic approaches to citizenship in his/her school.
> ➤ Each student should be able to **analyze** and **debate** the values of a democratic society.
> ➤ Each student should be able to **state why** democratic citizenship is beneficial to society.
> ➤ Each student should **participate** in democratic practice in his/her school.

Consider the following as a set of goals of teachers, parents, and the community for democratic schools:

Service to Others
> ➤ Each student will be a participating member of society.
> ➤ Each student will contribute his/her skills to making the community a better place to live.

Respect
- ➢ Each student will demonstrate integrity and honesty in moral principle and character.
- ➢ Each student will be truthful and demonstrate trustworthiness and responsibility.
- ➢ Each student will demonstrate cooperation, responsibility, compassion, and respect of self and others.

Learning
- ➢ Each student will demonstrate a desire to learn.
- ➢ Each student will acquire knowledge or skills, will study, and will become informed.

Standards for Teaching Social Studies—History

The National Board for Professional Teaching Standards (NBPTS) a non-profit, non-partisan organization supports the reform and commitment of American Education (1997, p. 1). In so doing, it has embarked on a mission to establish "high and rigorous" standards for accomplished teaching. As part of its reform of national goals, it has created standards that help teachers reflect on their teaching and demonstrate their own growth and development. In order to receive a certificate of accomplishment in these standards of Social Studies—History, an accomplished teacher must demonstrate a high level of "knowledge, skills, dispositions and commitments to practice." A Nationally Board Certified Teacher (NBCT) must demonstrate expertise in two dimensions: "the developmental level of the students and the subject or subjects being taught" (p. 4).

The Student Developmental Levels
- ◆ Early childhood, ages 3-8
- ◆ Middle childhood, ages 7-12
- ◆ Early adolescence, ages 11-15
- ◆ Adolescence and young adulthood, ages 14-18+

For the content area of Social Studies—History, a standards committee of broadly representative professionals has created standards for assessment for the prospective candidate for NBCT. These standards are organized into three sub-areas: Preparing, Advancing, and Supporting Student Learning (p. 18). An overview of the standards appears below:

Preparing for Student Learning
- ◆ Knowledge of Students—Forming constructive relationships with students.
- ◆ Valuing Diversity—Encouraging students to value self and others.
- ◆ Knowledge of Subject Matter—Using a broad knowledge of social studies and history to plan curriculum based on major concepts illuminated by history and social studies.

Advancing Student Learning

- ◆ Advancing Disciplinary Knowledge and Understanding—Using strategies and techniques that engage students' interest and understanding of United States history, world history, economics, political science, and geography.
- ◆ Promoting Social Understanding—Promoting the social aspects of the human condition, physical environment, cultural settings, and emerging trends for the future.
- ◆ Developing Civic Competence—Developing knowledge, skills, and attitudes needed to be a responsible citizen of a constitutional democracy.

Supporting Student Learning

- ◆ Instructional Resources—Selecting, adapting, and creating rich and varied resources for social studies and history.
- ◆ Learning Environments—Creating and fostering dynamic learning environments (i.e., trust, equity, risk taking, independence, and collaboration).
- ◆ Assessment—Using a variety of assessment methods to obtain useful information about students' learning and development.
- ◆ Reflection—Using reflection on their own practice, on students' performance, and on developments in their field.
- ◆ Family Partnerships—Demonstrating understanding and value of the role of parents and guardians.
- ◆ Professional Contributions—Demonstrating regular work with colleagues, at school, and in their field.

(National Board for Professional Teaching Standards, 1997, p. 18)

All of these standards play an important role in the life of a teacher and the teacher's portrayal of democratic practice. Several standards are explicit in their support of the themes of **LF, JF,** and **EEO** (a discussion of these themes can be found in Appendix A). These standards also can be explored more thoroughly in the NBPTS 1997 document (see Appendix B).

Of these standards, the following selective standards may serve as a focus for this workbook:

Standards for Emphasis in Observation

- ➤ Knowledge of Subject Matter
- ➤ Advancing Disciplinary Knowledge and Understanding
- ➤ Promoting Social Understanding
- ➤ Developing Civic Competence
- ➤ Reflection

A Few Words about Schools and Practice

Schools are places where we teach children about the values and expectations that the larger society has of its adult members. A school environment is one place where students learn the values of citizenship. After years of schooling, students begin to transfer the values of school citizenship to cultural, community, and country citizenship. To transfer and believe in democracy as a value or way of life, students must experience these values in their learning environment—the school setting. Consider the following statement about how students learn about democracy:

> *If people are to secure and maintain a democratic way of life, they must have opportunities to learn what that way of life means and how it might be led.*
> (Dewey, 1910)

What exactly is a democratic way of life? Consider the following three values in American democracy:

> Liberty and Freedom (**LF**)
> Justice and Fairness (**JF**)
> Equality and Equal Opportunity (**EEO**)

Are these values considered important in a democratic way of life? If so, how can schools help students learn in an environment that expresses these values in school life? That is, how can schools become democratic societies for students? If we create a democratic school, we may find that students will grow up with values of democracy as part of their way of thinking. This theme is found in the writing of Maxine Greene (1985, p. 40):

> *Surely it is an obligation of education in a democracy to empower the young to become members of the public, to participate, and play articulate roles in the public space.*

Adults can help by providing for schools that practice the values of a democracy, and teachers can extend these practices in their own classrooms. Teachers could reflect on their practice and ask of themselves as did Plato in *The Republic Book VIII:*

> *When a democracy which is thirsting for freedom has evil cupbearers presiding over the feast, and has drunk too deeply of the strong wine of freedom, then, unless her rulers are very amenable and give a plentiful draught (1), she calls them to account and punishes them, and says that they are cursed oligarchs.*
> (Loomis, 1942, p. 451)

Schools that are democratic must also realize that, by the very nature of promoting values such as freedom, the opportunity for non-democratic ideas may surface. Students and teachers alike may demand that some school practices feel less than free. For example, students who are required to wear school uniforms to public schools may feel that their First Amendment rights (free speech, free expression) are being subjugated to the community or majority will.

How can schools promote the democratic practice of freedom and still remain true to two of the other tenets of democracy: justice/fairness and equality/equal opportunity?

This text begins a journey about reflection on practice the practice of democratic schools!

To the Instructor

How to Use This Text

This text is written to help students observe and participate in classrooms using a democratic model of practice. Observation forms are organized under the following topic areas:

➢ Observation Guide and Forms—Part Two
➢ Classroom Instruction and Lesson Plans—Part Two
➢ Curriculum Projects, Activities, and Case Studies—Part Three
➢ Analyzing the Role of Citizenship in Democracy—Part Three
➢ Writing a Philosophy of Democratic Education Statement—Part Three

How to Use the Observation Forms

The observation forms are designed to guide students in reflection while in a field experience. Students are given tips on how to use the forms to take notes and observe a lesson plan. The forms contain focus questions related to the content of their observation. After the students take notes on their forms, they are encouraged to reflect on their observation by using the section of the form titled *Democratic Practice Reflection*. The forms may be used in individual or group reflection in a course or with the student's mentor-teacher.

Deciding on an Observation/Participation Sequence for Students

A sample three-semester observation format is found in Part One. Instructors may want to vary the topics of observation and discuss with their students what they would like to observe. It is suggested that the instructor encourage the use of this text for more than one semester or course so that students can observe several teaching models.

Tools for Student Use of the Democratic Practice Discourse Model for Observation/Participation

The following items in Part Two will help students use the model:

➢ Description of the use of the model
➢ Focus questions to guide the use of the model
➢ Graphic of the model
➢ Discourse/Democratic Practice Lesson Observation Form

Tips for Student Use of the Democratic Discourse Model of Observing

Observation encourages students and teachers to think about ways in which conversation is generated between participants in the classroom. For example, a teacher may think of trying the Socratic model of questioning. This model asking a question, expecting students to return an answer, and then probing the response of the student is one way that teachers use the discourse to focus on key points in a discussion. The democratic discourse model allows a student to observe and determine which of the historical/philosophical approaches a teacher uses in discourse in the classroom.

> ➤ Ask students to review the model and apply the model to their observations.
> ➤ Encourage students to meet with others in class and compare their use of the model.
> ➤ Suggest that students show their observation forms to their mentor-teachers for feedback and discussion.
> ➤ Use the model yourself and discuss your own teaching with your class.
> ➤ Draw upon your entire class's field experience and encourage a dialogue about the use of the model.

What to Expect from Students' Written Observations

When pre-service (PS) teachers observe in the classroom, they often watch the teacher's facility with classroom tasks such as where the teacher stands or how the teacher manages multiple efforts such as speaking and using an overhead projector. It is important that students become aware of their decisions of what they want to observe, as well as how those decisions affect their own practice (Wactler, 1999). Writing about one's observations is a form of self-discourse (Wactler, 1999) and is a statement about the teacher's philosophy that offers a format for the pre-service teacher to clarify his/her vision of the role of the teacher (Wactler, 1990). Reflection on teaching has been shown to be one of the most powerful tools for teachers to implement their philosophy of education (Wactler, 1990; Zeichner, 1987-1997).

The forms in this text are designed to focus students' attention on the classroom as well as the entire school site. In order to determine what to observe, or what to take notes about, students could consider

> ➤ The democratic discourse model of observation
> ➤ Their understanding of historical/philosophical orientations of democracy
> ➤ Their university coursework
> ➤ Their personal goals for learning this semester
> ➤ Their prior school experience

Repeating Observation Topics

The instructor may want to repeat an observation topic from a previous semester. Often topics are pre-assigned for a more in-depth observation. For example, the first semester a student, may observe direct instruction and notice that the teacher uses a certain format to facilitate instruction. The next semester, when the instructor has assigned observation of direct instruction, the instructor may want students to focus on resources and materials that align with giving clear instructions.

The observation forms for each topic may be used in every semester of the field experience and build on prior student knowledge.

The following sample semester observation format is one method of
organizing topics; however, repetition and re-organization
of observation topics are encouraged.

Sample Semester Observation Format

First-Semester Observations

➢ Small Group Instruction
  ♦ Direct instruction
➢ The Work Environment: Supplies and Resources
  ♦ Centers for exploring and creating
➢ Classroom Management
  ♦ Whose rules? The definition of a good citizen
➢ Applying Learning: Activities for Practice
  ♦ Worksheets books
  ♦ Book tests, reports, and text material
➢ Evaluation and Grading
  ♦ Portfolio grading
  ♦ Narrative evaluation
➢ Technology, Resources, and Special Programs
  ♦ Music, art, and physical education

Second-Semester Observations

➢ Large Group Instruction
  ♦ Direct instruction
  ♦ Discourse sections
➢ Small Group Instruction
  ♦ Pairs and practice
  ♦ Independent work
➢ Cooperative Learning
  ♦ How to decide on grouping students
  ♦ How to decide on the role of each student
➢ The Classroom Environment
  ♦ Seating arrangement
  ♦ Grouping students
  ♦ Multi-age
➢ The Work Environment: Supplies and Resources
  ♦ Centers for direct instruction

> Classroom Management
>   ◆ Breaking a rule
>   ◆ Particularity
>   ◆ Excusing a rule
>   ◆ Consequences
> Applying Learning: Activities for Practice
>   ◆ Technology and applied projects
>   ◆ Multi-media, tapes, video, and photos
> Evaluating and Grading
>   ◆ Using a percentage scale
>   ◆ Affective efforts: creativity, effort, and resources
>   ◆ Evaluating improvement
>   ◆ Improving one's grade—the extra credit-mastery model
> Technology, Resources, and Special Programs
>   ◆ Special education
>   ◆ Gifted education
>   ◆ Technology and computers (the Internet)
>   ◆ Media labs and libraries
> Adjunct Activities
>   ◆ What are the rules?
> School and District Policy
>   ◆ School rules
>   ◆ Room rules
> Community and Business Participation
>   ◆ Parent volunteers

Third-Semester Observations

> Types of Classroom Instruction
>   ◆ Critical thinking
>   ◆ Discovery learning—an inquiry model
> Cooperative Learning
>   ◆ Independent work
> The Classroom Environment
>   ◆ Grouping students
>   ◆ Tracking
>   ◆ Looping
>   ◆ Diversity issues: multi-cultural, bilingual, ESL programs
> Classroom Management
>   ◆ Reflecting on management—teacher as leader for citizenship

- ➢ Applying Learning: Activities for Practice
  - ◆ Homework and projects due
    - ▪ Purpose
    - ▪ Appropriate to objective
    - ▪ Evaluation
      - Student self-evaluation
      - Teacher evaluation
- ➢ Evaluation and Grading
  - ◆ Grading on a bell curve
  - ◆ Age/grade and content appropriateness
- ➢ Technology, Resources, and Special Programs
  - ◆ Language programs
  - ◆ Counselors—academic/career and special needs
- ➢ Adjunct Activities
  - ◆ Who participates in special events? Selecting students for team sports and the lead in the school play
- ➢ School and District Policy
  - ◆ District rules
  - ◆ Government and the law
- ➢ Community and Business Participation
  - ◆ Booster clubs and parent groups
  - ◆ Business partnerships

Using the Observation Forms

Students may use the **topic Observation forms** for *one or more observations*. They should use the space at the top right hand corner to enter the course topic, their name, the date of the observation, and the number of the observation such as first observation or second observation:

Sample Form
Date: September 18 Course: ECE: 571 Methods of Teaching Social Studies Observation #   1   Name: Thomas Smith Teacher Name: Mrs. Jones School Site: River Elementary School **Classroom Management Observation Form**   Reflection Notes and Summary:

Tips for the Instructor

> ➤ Students may choose to sit anywhere in the classroom when they take notes.
> ➤ Ask students to decide on a place where they can observe easily, but not interfere with the comfort of the students in the class.
> ➤ They should have a new form for each observation.

Part Two

A Guide to Observing and Participating in Schools

- **Chapter One**
  What to Expect at Elementary, Middle, and Secondary School Sites

- **Chapter Two**
  Observing with a Model for Democratic Discourse

- **Chapter Three**
  Types of Classroom Instruction

- **Chapter Four**
  Preparing to Participate in Classrooms

Chapter One

What to Expect at Elementary, Middle, and Secondary School Sites

Your placement at a school site may have been pre-arranged for you. The school secretary and principal usually will be expecting you. Be certain to phone the school before you appear at the site. If you know the teacher's name, leave a message with your phone number so he or she may set up a convenient time for you to visit the school. It is important to remember that many school-related events can all occur at a school office. You may find that you have to wait your turn to be helped, whether appearing in person or phoning the school.

Elementary Schools

School settings for grades K-6 are busy places. Parents are dropping off or picking up students. Teachers are on "duty" watching the busses arrive, cars come and go, and students enter the building. At the elementary school level, all students must be observed by certified personnel (aide, teacher, principal), so you will begin your observation in the front of a school. What do you notice? Are there rules for entering school? Do you know where to park your car? Do you need to sign in as a visitor? Do you need an identification badge? Are the students arriving at school in an orderly manner? Are they given rules to follow when they arrive? This type of observation is often termed field observation, or observing the field or context of operation (Wactler, 1990). Elementary schools are sensitive to knowing where students are at all times. Teachers are accountable for **where** students are.

Notice the way students walk down the halls and where they go first. Observe the students following school rules. Are they knowledgeable about the rules? For example, can they eat snacks in the hallways? Do they appear to think that the rules of behavior around the school grounds are **fair**? Do the rules appear to be applied to all students equally, **without particularity** (Soltis, 1992)? Sometimes a rule is applied to just one person. This is called "particularity" and requires that the teacher explain why the rule is applied in a certain manner. When you meet the teacher of an elementary school classroom, he/she usually explains the rules of the classroom so that you know the reasons behind the actions. Most students in grades K-6 are learning a great deal about **school citizenship**.

Once you meet your teacher, ask about schoolwide rules as well as classroom rules.

> Rules within classrooms may vary. A large part of developing classroom management for democratic citizenship is students' understanding that the rules are (a) made for the common good, (b) just and fair, and (c) equally applied.

Take notes about your first school site meeting:

School rules_____
_____
_____
_____
_____
_____
_____

Classroom rules_____
_____
_____
_____
_____
_____

Finally, the school **district** may have rules for all students within its jurisdiction. These may be **broader rules** and sound more like goals. For example, a district may have a rule that students may not disturb the learning environment in any manner.

Find out about districtwide rules and add these rules to your notes:

District rules_____
_____
_____
_____
_____
_____
_____
_____
_____
_____

Middle Schools

Middle school organization can vary by the grade level. Some middle schools are grades 6 through 8, and others are grades 7 and 8 only. Students may still arrive at school only in busses or the cars of their parents. The focus of many students is the interaction between students. The age grouping of students is part of school organization (e.g., sixth grades, or sixth grade team), but in this setting content areas such as mathematics or social studies is the second organizational theme to middle school. Thus, a school may organize its students in a sixth grade team of four predominant content areas: math, science, social studies, and language arts. For students of this type of school, rules pertaining to team expectations and community often predominate, and teacher teams may make decisions about classroom rules.

> In order to think about **democratic practice**, notice how **teacher teams** decide on rules for individuality/freedom, justice, fairness, equal opportunity/equality.

Middle school students move from classroom to classroom and have many different teachers during their day. In what ways are schools practicing the elements of democratic practice? Do all teachers think that the team rules are democratic? Should teachers make decisions as a team or individually? Which method of deciding on rules is more beneficial to students? Why?

Ask your middle school teacher teams about team rules and how they are created. Write your notes below:

School rules _____
_____
_____
_____
_____

Teacher team rules _____
_____
_____
_____
_____

District rules _____
_____
_____
_____

Secondary Schools

Secondary or high schools are most often aligned with a business model of organization. Students are often viewed by administrators as consumers, or clients, who have individual needs such as time or course needs. Typically, high schools are organized around the content in an organizational theme termed "departments." The individual recognized as the educational leader for a content department is called a **department chair** or **department coordinator**. Often, when you first report to a high school for placement, you are sent by the secretary to have a meeting with the department chair/coordinator. This individual usually has taught for many years and has observed multiple approaches to teaching.

When a department chair needs to meet with faculty, he/she organizes a faculty meeting and discusses problems that the department may be facing. Teachers usually are **independent and free** to make their own choices about classroom rules; however, when an issue begins to concern all the teachers, the team approach (as in middle schools, and sometimes even in elementary schools) is used to decide on rules that everyone may need.

If you attend a faculty meeting, be certain to listen to teachers' debates. Teachers value their freedom of choice in making rules and are usually very clear about their own approaches.

Ask the department chair to introduce you to many members of the department's faculty so you can learn about several approaches to classroom rules and decisions about the rules. Listen to the discussion about how teachers decide upon homework policy, late work, missed work, absences, or early release for student off-site jobs.

> Think about rules at the high school. Which rules appear to meet the value of **independence for the individual**? Which appear **fair and just**? Are the rules applied **equally**, giving all students an equal opportunity for success?

When speaking with the department chair, with your teacher, or at a department faculty meeting, take notes about how democracy applies in the decisions that are made:

Teacher rules_____

_____

_____

_____

Faculty/department rules_____

_____

_____

_____

District rules

_____

_____

_____

_____

Using the Observation Guide

> **Taking Observation Notes:**
> **Tips and Guidelines for Instructors and Students**

Taking observation notes is a first step in collecting data about your experiences at a school. Some of the places or events that you may want to use as a focus for your note taking are listed in the table of contents and include the following:

- ➢ Classroom instruction
- ➢ A practice or activity, either in the classroom or an extracurricular activity such as band practice
- ➢ Classroom environment
- ➢ Activities for practice
- ➢ Evaluation and grading
- ➢ Technology, resources, and special programs
- ➢ Adjunct activities such as the school play
- ➢ School and district policy
- ➢ Community and business participation

Guidelines

Most classrooms are organized around types of interactions, teacher to student, student to student, or students with teacher. Therefore, when you begin your observation, try to find a place to sit that does not interfere with the normal flow of discourse or conversation in these interactions. For example, when students are grouped around a small table for group reading with their teacher, the other students may be working (a) alone, (b) with a reading aide, (c) with a parent volunteer, (d) with a student teacher or another intern, or (e) independently in a small group. If you sit too closely to any of these groups, you may change the conversational environment for the students. If a student makes a mistake, he/she may wonder who you are and whether you heard the mistake. Thus, try to put some distance between yourself and the students you are observing.

Be prepared with your observation guide and a pen so you do not disturb the teacher's pacing of the lesson. Next, do not stop a lesson to have a teacher repeat the instructions, or to help you with the names of the students. You may conference with the teacher later.

Use your observation guide to focus your notes. If you want to focus your observation on seating arrangements and small group instruction, first try drawing the seating arrangement of students that you want to watch. Do not worry that you will not watch the entire class. You want to focus your observations so that you can find themes in the notes that **identify the democratic practice of teaching**.

After you draw the seating arrangement, see if you can **identify the steps to the lesson** (the instructional steps) modeled by the teacher. For example, in a reading lesson, the teacher may start by asking students about their own experience and then move into direct instruction of a reading skill such as defining vocabulary words. The students may then read the story silently, followed by the teacher asking questions about the story. Once you identify the steps to the lesson, **take purposeful notes** about the practices and activities, the questioning strategies, and the methods that appear to represent the three identifiable definitions of democratic practice (**LF, JF,** and **EEO**).

Observation of a Lesson

One of the ways to learn how to utilize teaching methods is to observe a teacher in a classroom. Observing and evaluating lessons can help you refine your own skills by allowing you to focus your attention on areas you may be working on in your university courses. You may want to observe a lesson with an emphasis on strategies for classroom management or techniques for asking higher-order questions. You may observe a new way to use mathematics manipulatives. Use the following observation guide to list all the elements of an observed lesson to practice observing for democratic practice.

Be certain to fully describe the classroom environment.

After the lesson, take time to reflect on your analysis of the teacher and the students. In the *observation of a lesson form,* use the section titled, *"reflection on democratic practice."* For your reflection, write your analysis of the strengths of the lesson and those areas that you would teach differently, supporting your response to both categories. Another way to reflect on an observed lesson is to review your observation form and make notes about areas that you feel would support the learning objective (reinforcement) and areas you would change (refine).

If possible, ask the classroom teacher for a lesson plan or curriculum guide. Also ask for copies of any guided practice such as a worksheet or map. Save these examples to retain with the observation form. Ask the classroom teacher for his/her reflection of the lesson. Note the areas of reinforcement and refinement in the evaluation section of the observation form.

Keep in mind that few, if any, lessons are ever perfect. Each lesson is an experience that draws on many factors—children's abilities, children's needs, school time, and setting among them. Thus, some lessons that you observe may be quiet or practice time, and others may be rather interactive and involve many strategies. All lessons are designed to help students reach an objective for a specified period of time (e.g., math objective today, reading objective today, etc.).

Lessons that are sequential and grouped to reach a curriculum goal are usually called a "unit." These lessons are sequential and follow steps that support students' understanding of several objectives. You may be observing one of several lessons in a unit. Lessons in a unit are often designed to meet district and state goals and standards. Thus, you may be observing only a very small part of the curriculum and should not be concerned that the lesson you are observing is not covering all the information about a topic.

When observing, be certain to sit where you can see the entire class (usually in the back of the room). You may take notes or script and translate your notes onto the observation form or, if you prefer, take your notes directly onto the form. The observation form should be legible when you complete it.

After you have completed your observation and have filled in the form for observation of a lesson, use the bottom section of the form to reflect on the lesson. This is called "reflection on democratic practice."

Each of the following themes may be used on your observation forms. You may place them on any section of the form to indicate an element of democratic practice. For example, when students peer coach after a spelling lesson, that step in the lesson may be identified with the symbol **EEO**. Students have an opportunity to learn from each other.

> **Use the Symbols for Each Theme in Democratic Practice**

LF - Liberty and Freedom

JF - Justice and Fairness

EEO - Equality and Equal Opportunity

Reflecting on your observation

Go back to the notes you have taken. Find the themes of each section of your notes by looking for the **symbols of LF, JF, and EEO.** In the reflection part of the form, write your reasons for thinking that an activity is labeled with a particular symbol. If you have changed your thoughts about the label, change the symbol and give your reason. In Part Three of this workbook, there are forms for analyzing each of these themes.

You should save your observation forms so that you can write about all the observed lessons of themes of **LF, JF, and EEO.** Your instructor may have other ways to organize your guide forms.

Tips

➤ Sit in a comfortable chair with some distance between you and the students.
➤ Have a pen or pencil ready.
➤ Use a focused observation guide.
➤ Take notes on the topic of the focused observation and do not include other topics.
➤ Use the symbols **LF, JF,** or **EEO** to identify themes of democracy.
➤ On the bottom part of the observation form, reflect on your lesson.
➤ Refer back to the symbols in your notes. Decide if the symbols that you used are still the symbols you think make sense for the observed practice.
➤ Summarize your reflection in a short paragraph.

Lesson Observation Form

Teaching Event 1: Observation of a teacher led event occurring during the "set" or introduction part of the lesson. Describe what the teacher has said and what strategies were used. What did the students say or do?

Teaching Event 2: Observation of a teacher led event occurring during instruction prior to a cooperative learning activity. Describe what the teacher has said and what strategies were used. What did the students say or do?

Democratic Reflection:

Observation of a Lesson:

1. Select one of the themes of democracy discussed in this text: **LF, JF, EEO.**
2. While thinking about one of these themes, observe the teacher's lesson and identify two separate instances where the teacher utilized **LF, JF,** or **EEO.** In the example above, the teacher used justice and fairness as a theme in the lesson during the set and during the instruction on how to work in cooperative learning groups.

Steps to Democratic Reflection:

1. Go back and review each teaching event. Describe the elements of the selected theme, (such as **Justice/Fairness JF**). Note: Use just one theme for each observation.
2. Write a reflection that summarizes how this theme was used and why it may be important to teaching and learning.
3. Write about your impression of the importance of this theme to your own teaching. Would you implement the lesson in the same manner as the teacher you have observed? Do you think the theme (such as justice) could be improved or designed to be used with students in another way?

Forms for Data Collection

Using the Forms

Forms for collecting data can be useful in gathering a quick view of the entire classroom or in finding a pattern or theme in the classroom. Use these forms to help you decide what types of themes are part of your teacher's practice. For example, how does the teacher give directions for a lesson? How are rules for classroom management explained?

Be certain to use the symbols **LF**, **JF**, and **EEO** after you look at the filled-in data sheet. Using these symbols will help you **identify the themes of democratic practice**.

Teacher and Student Form

The data collection form below is often used in large group discussion so the observation has as its focus a Socratic or two-way dialogue type of discussion. Often the teacher asks a question, follows the questions by a question to the class, leads the class through some type of large group discussion (often informational), then follows up with another question/response period. In order to capture the types of questions the teacher asks and how students respond, use the following form:

DATA COLLECTION FORM	
Teacher Dialogue	**Student Response**
Democratic Reflection	

Tips for Use of Teacher/Student Form

1. Write the noun and verb used.
2. Add unique or key words.
3. Add the **LF**, **JF**, and **EEO** symbols.
4. Summarize the dialogue by themes.
5. Write a reflection of this observation.

Questions to Guide Democratic Reflections

1. Who directed the questions? teacher? students?
2. What happened when a student did not answer the teacher's question correctly?
3. What happened when a student answered a question correctly?
4. Were students encouraged to challenge the teacher's answer?
5. Did the teacher present information that showed various perspectives?
6. Were students encouraged to solve their own problems?
7. Were students encouraged to be a risk taker and try out an answer, even if they failed?

Notes

Whole Group Form—Topical Focus

A whole group/topical form is used to gather data about various types of activities in the *entire* room. It is an overview of the whole group and can serve as a "snapshot" of what a class does during a certain time period of the day. For example, you may want to observe the morning opening routine of an elementary school classroom and determine how much of the routine is handled by students, how much is done by the teacher, and how much is student "off task" behavior. To determine the categories for your form, list those activities in a **key** or **legend** on your form, and use symbols to indicate the types of activity you will be noting, and where in the classroom the activity occurs. You may also want to use a timed form that shows when, during the observation, the observed activity occurs. A topical form may also be used to focus on just *part* of the group. This is called a "focused topical form."

Topical Form

Whole Group—Morning Routine

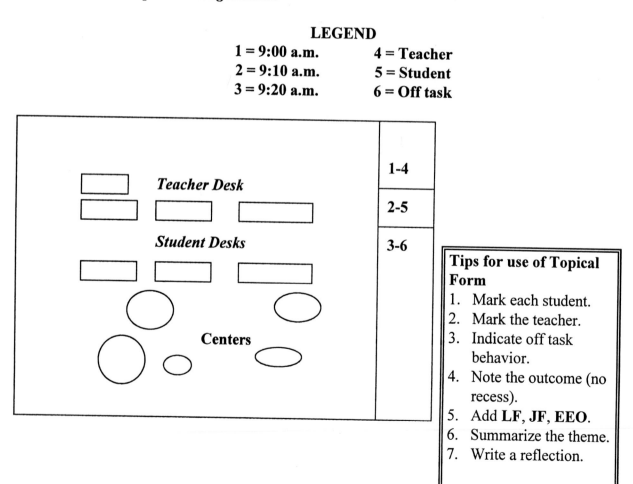

LEGEND

1 = 9:00 a.m.	4 = Teacher
2 = 9:10 a.m.	5 = Student
3 = 9:20 a.m.	6 = Off task

Tips for use of Topical Form
1. Mark each student.
2. Mark the teacher.
3. Indicate off task behavior.
4. Note the outcome (no recess).
5. Add **LF**, **JF**, **EEO**.
6. Summarize the theme.
7. Write a reflection.

Questions to Guide Democratic Reflections

1. What did the teacher say or do to begin the morning routine? What time was it? Were students encouraged to participate in the routine? How?
2. What happened when students became off task? What time was it? Were they encouraged to become part of the group?
3. What did the teacher say or do to respond to off task behavior?

Notes

Chapter Two

Observing with a Model for Democratic Discourse

Democratic Discourse Model

This model proposes that, for students to experience democracy and achieve well in an educative setting, schools need to recognize that their authority is generated from the community at large, a community that recognizes and should institute collaboration about how and what children learn. Therefore, the model presented in this text encourages a broad spectrum of resources for teachers and the community to use to educate students. The decision of who should control schools is part of society's interest in compulsory education; that is, the control of schools also tells us what it is that we want students to know about society.

When you observe schools and teachers for democratic practice, notice the parts of this model that you emphasize, and those parts that you use less. You may want to experiment with your focus and decide upon various elements of the model for different observations, or even for different semesters. For example, you may decide that one semester you want to emphasize using the elements of technology, multi-media, and student abilities as a focus of your observations. You may decide another semester to focus on the scope and sequence of curriculum and achievement tests as your venue.

In any case, your discourse with students, and theirs with you, will change through *your* lens of and your approach to teaching what you want to teach, as well as how you view the role of the learner. Ultimately, your opportunity and the opportunity of your students to converse about school will determine the shape of democratic practice in your classroom.

The art of using any model is realizing that not everyone uses a model in quite the same manner. As described by Peter Oliva (1992), planning to teach by thinking about curriculum itself is one way to begin to think about your approach to teaching. Others (Oliva, 1992) begin their plan with curriculum goals for the students to achieve (Tyler, 1949).

In any case, the elements of emphasis and use of the model **are the art of teaching**, and the outcome of this art is the opportunity for students to experience their teacher's vision of democratic practice.

Questions to Guide the Use of the Model

1. What area of the model did you want to emphasize when you observe in your school? the classroom? a teacher? the students?
2. What types of discourse did you observe?
3. How was the curriculum decided upon?
4. How was curriculum evaluated?
5. What opportunities existed for student and teacher interaction?
6. How was achievement measured?
7. Did you observe elements of democracy? (Label each element **LF**, **JF**, and **EEO.**)

How to Use the Discourse Model for Democratic Practice

Purpose of the Model

This model is designed as a tool to reflect upon and then gather the resources needed to design curriculum units, write lesson plans, and evaluate the implementation of teaching. The model has two main components: school practice and theory. Both sections are aligned with a main theme of democracy. The model uses one of the themes in this text, liberty and freedom, as a sample application. However, the model could be followed using any other theme, such as justice/fairness or equality/equal opportunity. The lateral or central line of the model shows Liberty and Freedom as the curricular goal.

The top of the model is titled "school practice" and describes elements of teacher classroom decision making (such as identifying a case study or problem, content areas that may align with the case, and methods to select from in curriculum design). The bottom part of the model is theoretical and offers teachers some suggestions for reflection and decision making. For example, the bottom suggests ways to think about social needs, philosophical orientation, and individual need. This section encourages each teacher to decide upon classroom practice based on a review of historical approaches or orientations to teaching.

Teachers create lessons and curriculum plans based on a large set of information. Some of this information can be organized through the discourse model as you think about the goals you have for democratic practice.

The sample model uses the theme of liberty/freedom as a curriculum goal. The instructional goal is the content area of Environmental Awareness, Appreciation, and Conservation. The model shows that there are many decisions to make concerning the organization of information and instruction for this unit.

Decisions about curriculum and practice are determined using the resources at each school, reflection on practice, and theory.

Step One:
Read Part Three, Chapter Four: How to Write a Philosophy of Democratic Education.

Step Two:
Determine if your orientation to teaching is most likely to be executive, humanist, classicist, or informationist.

Step Three:
Review the elements of the discourse model for democratic practice.

Components of the Model

➤ Democratic Practice Focus: Liberty/Freedom, Justice/Fairness, Equality/Equal Opportunity
➤ School Practice
➤ Theory

Step Four:
Review each component of the discourse model and select those components needed to design your lesson plans and curriculum unit.

Selecting a Democratic Practice Focus

Appendices B and C contain historical background regarding notions of democratic practice.

In Appendix B, the historical information explores notions of why a perspective such as liberty adds to the well-being of members of a society. Given a review of the historical basis for decision making, teachers can determine which focus (**LF**, **JF**, or **EEO**) may be needed in order to organize the teaching components in their rooms. Read this section and determine if you will use **LF**, **JF**, or **EEO** as a focus for preparing a curriculum unit or lesson.

Appendix C is a set of qualitative tables that show individuals in history and their main themes or contributions to a topic of **LF**, **JF**, or **EEO**. Review the table that you have selected for your theme. If you have selected the theme **LF**, review that table and select an individual that has a concept that contributes to your thinking about democratic practice.

School Practice

The top section of the model contains the following sub-sections.

Case study sample: The students at River Elementary School are careless with cafeteria food. They throw out much of their lunch and argue with the yard-duty teachers. The faculty wants to focus the campus and create a sense of school community. How can you build a collaborative environment? What units of study focus on the relationships of people and their community?

Individual Needs	Develop a case study and a curriculum goal that could be used as a response to the case. Identify a student need for your case.
Content Areas	Select a content area(s) that supports the curriculum goal. Thematic planning may include several content areas, such as social studies and literature.
Methods	Review methods such as direct instruction or discovery learning and list those methods that you will use in your unit.
Classroom Practice	Determine which practices you will use. Practice sessions such as large or small group activities may vary according to your goals for students.
Resources	Identify the resources available at your school or district. Reflect on the availability of resources for classroom use. Access? Censorship? Ethical use? Materials, books, media?
Evaluation	Review methods of evaluation. Align these methods with your curriculum goal in democratic practice. What input do students or parents have in curriculum design? What are the district/school guidelines? When do you use formative or summative evaluation measures of attainment? What type(s) of evaluation?
Revision	Reflect on the goals and outcomes of your unit. How would you change this unit? When do you revise your plan?

Theory

The bottom part of the model contains the following sub-sections.

Social Needs   Develop a case study that centers on social need. Align a curriculum goal with this case.

Curriculum Model   Review state and district curriculum goals. Follow steps of a curriculum model, such as the Oliva, Taba, or Tyler model (see Appendix D).

Philosophy of Education   Review the orientations of teaching presented in Part Three, Chapter Four. State your preferred philosophy in such areas as the role of the teacher and the goals of education. Which orientation best describes the role of the student?

Theory and Historical Perspective   Review the historical perspectives in Appendix B. Determine which definition of a theme of democracy (such as **LF**) supports your curriculum goal. Reflect on the historical understanding of this perspective. Review the qualitative table (Appendix C) that presents information for each theme. Find an individual in history that has a sub-theme that supports your goal for a democratic classroom. The model shows John Dewey and his methods for humanist/progressive education.

Discourse Model for Democratic Practice

Practice

Individual Needs	Content Areas	Methods	Classroom Practices and Activities	Resources	Evaluation Model(s)	Revisions
• Students need to build a sense of school as community • Outcome: To gain an appreciation for community such as wildlife in its natural habitat	• Science • Social Science • Language Arts • Art • Math	• Unit plan: Nine lesson unit on environmental concerns • Short-term plan: This would fit into a month-long science/social science unit on life studies • Extended long-term plan: Develop a year-long plan • Resources: Books, posters, videos, commercial resources, museum field trips, speakers, Internet • Lesson plans	• Small group work • Cooperative learning • Whole group work • Individual • Analytic methods • Technology: Research and word processing • Inquiry/discovery methods	• Use a local newspaper • Use a curriculum text, such as Oliva, P. • *Navajo Longwalk*, Armstrong • *Do Arizona*, Spanish Publication • *Philosophy of Education Workbook*, Stamm and Wactler	• Checklists • Rubrics • Quizzes • Self/peer evaluation (presentations throughout unit) • Portfolios • Videotape • Web page	• After unit has been taught (summative) • During the time unit is taught (formative) • With teachers and students • With parents and community

Curriculum Goal: Liberty/Freedom

Theory

Social Needs	Curriculum Model	Philosophy of Education	Theory and Historical Perspective
• Environmental awareness, appreciation, and conservation: The depletion of Arizona's environment (natural resources, wildlife, and culture) is a problem due to lack of awareness and conservation • Government (national and local) is becoming proactive • Educators are designing curriculum by including environmental issues	• One suggested text is *Developing the Curriculum*, Oliva, P., 1992 • Teacher reviews state, district curriculum • Teachers create teaching-learning units for their students by thinking about their students' interests and abilities • Teachers find interesting and relevant resources • A curriculum unit emerges	• Teacher as facilitator • Student as self-directed learner (Soltis, 1998; Stamm and Wactler, 1997) • Environment is rich with many resources for students • Focus on self-actualization and exploration • Emphasis on the role of the learner	**John Dewey** • Learn by doing • Experience as teacher • Progressive model • Creativity and exploration lead to an innovative and strong economy

(Pryor, 1999)

The following form may be used to observe with a focus on discourse in a classroom setting. The flow of discourse could be written on all sections of the form and the analysis of discourse as democratic practice could be completed on the reflection section of the form.

Discourse/Democratic Practice Observation Form

Name:
Date:
Observation #:
School:
Mentor-Teacher:

Objective of the Lesson*:

Anticipatory Set: What is the motivation, activation of prior knowledge, or introduction to the lesson?

Instructional Input: What are the instructional steps used in the lesson?

Check for Understanding: What strategies or techniques does the teacher use to question or check what the students know or **want to know**?

Guided Practice: How do the students practice the expected performance?*

Evaluation: What strategies does the teacher use to determine what the students have learned?

Closure: What strategies does the teacher use to determine what the students have learned?

Materials and Resources: What types of materials are used?

Classroom Interaction and Management: What are the strategies used?

Democratic Reflection of the Lesson
Find the themes of **LF, JF,** and **EEO.**
How was **discourse** used in each theme?
What was **effective**? What would you **change**?

Teacher's Lesson Plan
If you have a copy of the plan, note the elements of the plan on your form.
* Use of Democratic Discourse
Throughout the lesson, identify the themes of democratic practice, **LF, JF, and EEO** for each session.
* Reading aloud? Working together? Games? Independent work? Teacher/Student work?

Chapter 3

Types of Classroom Instruction

When you observe in the classroom, the teacher will draw upon many types of instruction. Read through the following section to become acquainted with the format of many types of instruction.

Your teacher may vary the type of instruction according to (a) an overall approach or philosophy of education (Soltis, 1992; Wactler, 1998); (b) the experience, abilities, or interests of the students (Boyd, 1962; Downs, 1975; Gardner, 1993); or (c) the objective of the lesson (Hunter, 1971).

Sources that additionally influence types of instructional implementation are (a) the subject matter, (b) each individual student, or (c) the community (Oliva, 1992). Adding to this list of strategies, Oliva further suggests the following considerations when deciding on instructional strategies:

> ➤ The time available
> ➤ The resources available
> ➤ The facilities available
> ➤ The objective (including district and state objectives)

Finally, **consider strategies of democratic practice** when deciding on types of instruction (Wactler, 1997, 1998). Review Appendix B of this text for a consideration of perspectives of the roots of democracy. Review historical figures that define democracy and their perspectives. Then think about instructional strategies such as cooperative learning or large group instruction.

For example, in writing about the consent of the governed, in 1690 John Locke (Lamprecht, 1928) emphasized the input of the governed in their own control over the organization of their nation and community. What is the role of the student in curriculum design? How do you consider the writing of Locke in your curriculum unit or lesson plans? Do you think students may want to have some input into how instruction is organized?

> Think about the symbols of **LF, JF,** and **EEO**.
> How do you implement those symbols in this process of deciding on instructional type?

The purpose of this overview is for you to be able to view instructional choices as part of democratic practice. You can reflect on the reasons a teacher chooses certain strategies in the classroom. Be certain to note in the **instructional input section of your observation forms** which choices are **LF, JF,** and **EEO**.

Large Group Instruction

Large group instruction can be called a production model (Soltis, 1992). It is an efficient model that is often used in school districts as a means to educate large numbers of students. Oliva (1992) wrote that proponents of group instruction point out that, for some purposes, teaching entire groups is more efficient and practical in our mass educational system than attempting to individualize instruction (p. 428). The efficiency of large group instruction lies in the focused and direct manner of the teacher and the ability of the teacher to assure that instruction proceeds in a clear, well-paced manner (Cruickshank, 1988).

Be certain to focus on elements of **LF, JF,** and **EEO** as you read the strategies of direct instruction below.

Direct Instruction

Instruction of a whole group in a direct manner involves lesson planning that has the attainment of an objective as its primary objective.

Strategies for Direct Instruction

➢ Stating a desired learner outcome
➢ Providing feedback to students
➢ Maintaining positive classroom behavior
➢ Managing disruptive behavior
➢ Beginning a lesson effectively
➢ Presenting information clearly
➢ Giving clear directions and explanations
➢ Promoting student retention and understanding
➢ Using effective closure and summarization

- ➤ Using effective instructional material
- ➤ Appropriating effective use of time
- ➤ Possessing knowledge of subject
- ➤ Managing classroom environment for teaching and learning.

(Enz, Cook, and Matani 1998; Oliva, 1992;
Cruickshank, 1988)

Critical Thinking

Critical thinking, or the inquiry model of instruction, is based on a Socratic or questioning model. (Strike, 1989). A teacher uses this strategy to guide a large group in thinking about an issue or a process. For example, in a math lesson, a teacher may ask the group, "Why did I multiply these two numbers?" In so asking, the teacher is expecting that the students will think through the steps that have been previously discussed and will respond with the correct reason. The logic of the process is important to the teacher along with the correct response. Thus, as in the questioning strategies of Socrates (Smith, 1984), the question of "why" leads the group to understand the correct answer.

Strategies for Critical Thinking

- ➤ Stating a desired learner outcome
- ➤ Addressing a single level of knowledge
- ➤ Providing feedback (vis-à-vis more questioning) to students
- ➤ Presenting information clearly
- ➤ Giving clear directions and explanations
- ➤ Using student responses and questions in instruction
- ➤ Using effective closure and summarization
- ➤ Promoting individual student learning
- ➤ Using teaching methods appropriately and effectively
- ➤ Demonstrating knowledge of subject

(Enz, Cook, and Matani 1998; Oliva, 1992; Strike,
1989)

Discourse

Discourse as instruction of a whole group often is observed as part of a teacher's repertoire of questioning strategies. However, other forms of discourse (communication) can be identified as a teacher-led skill in promoting student understanding of a content area (NCTM, 1991) as well as teacher understanding of the "value of the thinking of all students" (Sharp & Burton, 1998, p. 51). It has been well documented that teachers need to develop skill regarding how to use discourse as a precise and interpersonal manner of communication (Ball, 1991; Hess & Short, 1995; Schram & Rosaen, 1996).

Teachers often lead students through the process of **thinking about their thinking** and in so doing become **reflexive** in their approach to whole group instruction. Reflexive teaching means that the teacher presents thoughts about **how and why** an answer or a reason is stated, and the listener (usually the student) responds with his/her own answer or thoughts. **Democratic practice** in classrooms, with strategies of discourse, can be an opportunity for shared power with implications for both school (Wactler, 1990, 1997a, 1997b) and society (Strike, 1989; Soltis, 1992; Wactler, Stamm, Freeman, and Maldonado 1997).

In the case of **how a teacher shares power within a classroom**, a teacher can begin to create a basis for individual freedom (Jefferson, 1944) with the following strategies for instruction.

Strategies for Discourse

➤ Share your own beliefs and opinions.
➤ Ask what, how and why questions.
➤ Take risks (in your narrative and questions).
➤ Hypothesize.
➤ Make mistakes.

(Vacc, 1993)

➤ Provide for active participation in learning.
➤ Encourage students to write about and express ideas with a focus on clarity.
➤ Support the development of communication skills for democratic responsibilities of United States citizenship.
➤ Connect new concepts to previous ones to gain insight.
➤ Create new ideas and test them out.
➤ Develop confidence to take risks.
➤ Believe in the contributions (of students).
    (Graduate student 1, Northern Arizona University /Elementary Education, 1998)

Discovery Learning

Theorists such as Piaget (1926) and Havighurst (1972) have held that children develop in an unfolding sequence and follow stages of development that are promoted by their own opportunity to discover the world (Morrison, 1993). Discovery learning has been discussed by educators long before contemporary instructional plans included time and effort toward students' demonstration in their own knowledge of the world (Rousseau, 1962; Dewey, 1910; Downs, 1975; Jackson, 1996). Considered a progressive and a leader among those who support a child's effort to create and discover knowledge, John Dewey's impressive writings (1910-1950) have given educators a substantive background in understanding the link between **self-knowledge** (discovery) and **democracy** (see Democracy and Education, 1916) and **freedom**.

In contemporary terms, discovery learning is also termed the "constructivist" model, as students are given the opportunity to **construct thinking about knowledge in their own independent manner**.

Reflect on the example below about how students learn in a discovery or constructivist model.

Using Technology for Journal Writing

Objective:
> ➤ Students will be able **to demonstrate** their knowledge of areas such as the American Revolution, the rain forest, or math multiples and write a paper using the computer as a resource.

Set:
> ➤ Students will predict the future of society based on their topic and then as a group, determine elements of the writing process.
> ➤ **Students brainstorm** about writing a futuristic story on the computer.

Procedure:
> ➤ **Students peer edit** their rough drafts with their partner and use **analysis and discourse** in reflecting on their papers.
> ➤ Students use the computer to transpose their rough draft.
> ➤ Teacher leads **discussions** about **a variety of computer tools** to reason, make connections, solve problems, and communicate in groups and in peer edit pairs.
> ➤ Students **decide on** graphic for their paper.

Assessment:
> ➤ Students print out final paper and read aloud with their partner and other peers.

Strategies for Discovery Learning

➤ Promote students' ability **to define and solve problems.**
➤ Encourage **self-discipline, personal goals, and self-chosen tasks.**
➤ Facilitate **group planning, cooperative efforts, and shared leadership.**
➤ Teach **discourse**—speaking, writing, graphic expression and comprehension of others.
➤ Model and promote **mathematical reasoning** such as classification and quantification.
➤ Engage personal **talent and energy**...in skills and abilities.
➤ Represent **openness in points of view.**
➤ Utilize an **inquiry spirit.**
➤ Help cultivate **lifelong learning.**

(*High Scope Curriculum* in Morrison, 1993)

Small Group Instruction

Small group instruction centers on the effort of specific interests or skills. For example, a reading group or group project such as working on a play may involve a teacher working only with a small group. The group that is not working with the teacher is typically engaged in various types of other projects such as (a) extra activities in art, music, or physical education; (b) practice activities such as independent seat work with handouts; (c) a similar activity such as reading, but with the guidance of a teacher's aide; (d) a center; or (e) other activities in another room.

In any case, small group instruction requires that a teacher focus only on the individual needs of the small group, leaving or providing for the rest of the class in alternative instruction/practice. Small group instruction can be linked to the progressive philosophy of meeting the needs of the individual child (Morrison, 1993; Oliva, 1992; Soltis, 1992; Stamm & Wactler, 1997).

Direct Instruction

Direct instruction in small groups can promote a perspective that the teacher views each student in a **fair and just manner.** The teacher spends a focused amount of time with **just a few of the students** and the goal of this type of instruction is to promote both humanistic (self-actualization) and behaviorist (goal attainment) philosophies (Stamm & Wactler, 1997).

Strategies for Direct Instruction—Small Group

➢ Use a **separate physical area**, such as a table, desk, carpeted seated area.
➢ Be certain you have included the **entire group**.
➢ Include elements of **both goal attainment and personal self-satisfaction** in the lesson.
➢ Have resources **easily available**.
➢ Spend time giving feedback to each student.
➢ Prepare for **independent** demonstration of understanding and practice.

Pairs and Practice

Practicing in pairs, peer editing, and small group practice can be fun for students! A more focused type of cooperative learning (learning from and with one or more persons), small group practice is a type of practice that encourages the skills of each of the participants. For example, in writing about the progressive inquiry model and the ideas of John Dewey (1859-1952), Morrison (1993) writes that it was Dewey who believed that **the best preparation for democratic living** was for children to experience it through a process of schooling and reflective thinking (p. 127). Morrison lists the benefits of group learning as

➢ Positive independence
➢ Verbal (discourse) face-to-face interaction
➢ Individual accountability
➢ Social skills
➢ Group processing

(Morrison, 1993, p. 129)

To achieve, Morrison reports, pairs or groups need to ascertain that they are setting and meeting goals and that they are accountable for their goals.

Notes

Strategies for Paired or Small Group Practice

Reading

- ➢ Reading to another student
- ➢ Literature studies and read aloud
- ➢ Journal writing and peer editing
- ➢ Cross ability pairing, such as a fast reader with a slower reader
- ➢ Library time
- ➢ Cross grade level pairing for motivation and support (for example, fourth grader listens to first grader read)

Math

- ➢ Math manipulatives or flash cards
- ➢ Worksheets and peer correction

Small Groups

- ➢ Interest centers and practice/discussion
- ➢ Lab partners for middle or secondary courses
- ➢ Computer pairing for peer support

Projects

- ➢ Project preparation such as map making or dioramas
- ➢ Many hands-on activities such as art or music
- ➢ Science projects at all levels—for example, science fair projects or campaign posters for student council in secondary education

Independent Work

Some of the work accomplished in small groups or pairs is also practiced in a parallel manner, or side-by-side next to another person. For example, two students may be working in a peer-to-peer edit but first may want to write alone with their writing buddy sitting near them to brainstorm or advise. This type of practice can be supportive of the paired model and still provide for independent achievement. A teacher may want to incorporate some **independent work** into the model for paired practice.

Cooperative Learning

Several definitions of cooperative learning have been formulated around the practice of grouping students for cooperative effort. Morrison (1993) writes that cooperative learning is the term used for grouping students together for the purpose of helping one another study and learn. Peter Oliva (1992) reports that the Robert Slavin (1988) model of cooperative learning is focused on students helping each other **learn academic material.** Further, Oliva reports, Slavin encouraged **group rewards** for achievement. Johnson and Johnson conducted studies regarding the outcomes of cooperative learning, concluding that neither competition nor individualized instruction was more successful (in a general manner) than cooperative situations. Citing the outcome derived from groups is often high skill in higher-order thinking such as induction and performance on subsequent texts (Morrison, 1993).

Grouping Students

Cooperative learning groups are larger than pairs and usually about four to six students. Morrison writes that groups are structured by the teacher to include a balance of high- and low-achieving students with a variance between boys and girls, ethnicity and backgrounds (Morrison,1993).

For elements of **LF, JF,** and **EEO,** it is important for the teacher to consider the organization of these groups.

Morrison (1993) again draws on the work of Slavin to assess the effect of cooperative learning grouping. The implications of grouping on students appears to be

➢ High academic achievement
➢ High-level cognitive learning
➢ Strong positive effect on ethnic relationships
➢ Consistent effect on mutual concern among students
➢ Generally greater liking of school

(p. 431)

The Role of the Student

In a cooperative group, students learn to take responsibility for various tasks. Part of this responsibility is to share what they have learned with other members of the group (Morrison, 1993). **The teacher has a great deal of flexibility** in how he/she wants to organize groups and if and when he/she wants to change this organization. He/she also has **flexibility** in assigning grades. For example, a teacher may assign a group and/or an individual grade based on both achievement and individual effort (Morrison, 1993; Slavin, 1977-1983; Johnson and Johnson, 1975-1980).

Reflect on elements of democratic practice that include **LF**, **JF**, and **EEO** when you think about how grades are given.

Sometimes grades represent the amount of progress a student has made; sometimes the group suffers due to the lack of motivation of group members. Further, a grade may depend on **the type of role** a student has played. Consider the various roles the student can play in cooperative learning.

➢ **Organizer** - oversees the tasks of the group
➢ **Recorder** - handles records and paperwork
➢ **Procurer** - is responsible for materials and supplies
➢ **Reporter** - tells the entire class the results of the group's findings or project

Strategies for Grouping

Organize groups by:
- ➤ Experience with content
- ➤ Ability or interests
- ➤ Grade
- ➤ Verbal or social abilities

Strategies for Grading

- ➤ Has the **student** shown **improvement**?
- ➤ Has the **student** demonstrated **high achievement**? Met goals?
- ➤ Has the **group** shown **improvement**?
- ➤ Has the **group** met standards of **high achievement**? Met goals?
- ➤ How has the **group worked together previously**?

Independent Work

Is additional explanation needed regarding independent work in cooperative learning?

Take some notes that reflect on the effect of elements of democratic practice and cooperative learning. Use the symbols of **LF**, **JF**, and **EEO** to focus your thoughts.

Notes

Observation Form for Classroom Instruction

Focus on elements of LF, JF, and EEO.

Large Group Instruction

                                  Direct Instruction

    Critical Thinking

    Discourse

    Discovery/Inquiry Learning

Small Group Instruction

                                    Direct Instruction

    Pairs and Practice

Cooperative Learning

                                    Student Grouping Patterns

    Role of the Student

    Grading

Democratic Practice Reflections

The Classroom Environment

Seating Arrangement

Look around the classroom. There are probably several types of places where students can work. In elementary schools, the pattern for seating arrangements may vary according to grade level, age of students, student ability, and group interaction. The elementary classroom has desk space as well as work stations and interest centers. In secondary classrooms, the focus is usually on desk space, with some laboratory seating also available. Secondary classrooms, similar to special areas such as art or music have a content focus, and the seating needs may vary. Overall, most teachers decide on their own classroom seating, often varying the seating, taking into account such elements as class size and available types of resources such as desk size or shape.

When thinking about **democratic practice** and the elements of **IF, JF,** and **EEO**, think about the outcome of seating students in individual desks, in rows, or in small groups of tables. How about seating in round tables?

The teacher's desk also needs to be placed. Some teachers do not want a formal desk and work only from the cupboard area. Others prefer a desk at the front of the classroom or near the door.

Think about issues such as **privacy, freedom,** and **individual need.**[*] Do you think a person's desk should be private? Should your desk be private? Should students have access to materials on your desk? Should you have access to their desks?

Enz writes that some of the following elements of seating (1997) have been found to be part of the consideration veteran teachers give to room arrangement. In thinking about where to seat students, Enz also suggests thinking about the time of year for seating. For example, at the beginning of a school year, students seated near the teacher are more likely to have a sustained attention span. Further, the traffic flow of a room may also impede the attention span of students, as walking around multiple desks or tables can slow down a student's walk from one part of the room to another.

Strategies for Seating

> ➢ Sight line around the room
> ➢ Teacher observation around the room
> ➢ Traffic flow and clear space
> ➢ Instructional match (for issues of democratic practice—**LF, JF, EEO.**)

(Enz, 1997)

---

[*] Teachers' work space—easy access

Grouping Students

Reflect also on **LF, JF,** and **EEO** in thinking about how students are grouped. Are they **tracked or placed together in a pre-determined manner such as by ability, age, or achievement?** Are they grouped with **several ages and grades together in** a manner termed **multi-age grouping?** Do they start in a grade together with others in their **same age/group** and **stay with their teacher** for more than one year (such as grades 2 and 3), moving on to the following grade (such as grade 4 and their teacher **loops back** to grade 2 again)?

Each of these philosophies of grouping is representative of assumptions about how students may learn best and about issues of **what is best for an individual, just or fair,** or **equal** are part of the way schools implement **democratic practice.**

Strategies for Grouping

➢ What are the test scores for the group?

➢ How many students are new to the school?

➢ How well do you know the curriculum for each grade?

➢ What philosophy or approach to teaching do you hold?*

➢ What are the goals of the school and district?

➢ What are the goals and expectations of the parents in the community?

*See Part Three, Chapter 4, for further description of philosophies of education.

Diversity in Grouping

Teachers often approach diversity in grouping of students as the opportunity for inclusion of students with multiple abilities and perspectives. Students can experience becoming familiar with people of various needs and abilities. Students in schools that approach grouping with a diverse classroom include students with special needs (physical and emotional), language diversity and academic attainment in a learning community for the support and value of each student's special and unique contribution to the world. The right to a free and appropriate public education in the least restrictive environment is secured by the Education for all Handicapped Children Act of 1975 (amended 1986 and 1992), and re-authorizes the Individuals with Disabilities Education Act of 1991 and 1997 (Enz, 1997). Lyons and Rutowski wrote that special education has been interpreted as a continuum of educational placements and range from most restrictive to the least, the regular classroom (Enz, 1997).

A diverse and regular classroom may be composed of students from a wide range of backgrounds and abilities and be so grouped to provide for *individual need (IF), support of the common good (JF), and equal education (EEO).*

Strategies for Diversity in Grouping

➢ Review the Individual Educational Plan (IEP) for special needs students.
➢ Review the test scores for all students.
➢ Find out about community skills and abilities.
➢ Encourage student-to-student skills such as language tutoring.
➢ Ask for parental, business, and community volunteers for student support.
➢ Consider school, district, and state goals.
➢ Use multiple resources such as computer searches for additional information.
➢ Become skilled at writing lesson plans that meet the needs of all students.
➢ Include students themselves in your planning.
➢ Consider the physical plant of your school site.
➢ Consider the resources and funding (such as grants) that are available.

Notes

Supplies and Resources

Centers for Exploring and Creating

Students can experience and create their own curriculum and projects. Often they find they have learned a great deal from their hands-on work. John Dewey (1859-1952) promoted a model of student-centered curriculum, linking student interest with the direct goals of independence in a democratic nation (Dewey, 1910). Another type of center, one that often fosters practice is a center with behaviorist (Stamm and Wactler, 1977), or outcome-based goals. Both types of centers are limited to small groups usually 3-6 students and usually have all materials contained in a regulated space in the classroom.

When we think about how space is used, the resources provided, and the intent or goals of the center, we also need to **reflect on issues of LF, JF, and EEO**. Review the strategies below for some ways to **think about democratic practice**.

Strategies for Centers for Exploring and Creating

➤ Provide an area that is defined by a separate physical space such as a table, an area rug, or a few beanbag chairs.

➤ Select a wide variety of materials within the content area such as multiple tapes, a large bookcase of books, many types of Legos.

➤ Find motivating and innovative materials, such as a variety of, or shapes or new uses for familiar items.

➤ Secure materials that support and extend a lesson such as a variety of leaves to identify in a biology lab or a variety of maps for a history class in secondary education.

➤ Establish policies for use of the center. Think about who can use the centers. Why? When? How? (groups? independent?)

➤ What expectations or outcomes do you have?

➤ Ask for donations (community, parents, and students) of materials, and review the donations for appropriate use.

➤ Determine whether or not a grade or credit will be given for using a center.

➤ Add the use of technology to your center and set standards and expectations for this use.

Strategies for Direct Instruction in Centers

➤ Determine your goals for instruction in a center and be clear to the students.
➤ Have all materials immediately available.
➤ Communicate the expected work format, such as independent work on a project or worksheet.
➤ Prepare students for the independent work, prior to their working alone.
➤ Tell students about the grading policy.
➤ Expect students to be able to work alone.
➤ Use technology to support your center.
➤ Provide for multiple levels of knowledge by clarifying the steps or procedures students are to follow.

Classroom Management

Whose Rules? Classroom Citizenship and Responsibility

How are rules of order established in a classroom? How should they be established in society? What role should government play? What about the role of the teacher in establishing classroom management? While many books about strategies for management have been written, it is important to reflect on the elements of **LF**, **JF**, and **EEO** as you read about these strategies and underlying theoretical assumptions. Further, your own philosophy of education and approaches to classroom environment will also determine which of the styles of classroom management will provide your students with an opportunity to be part of a classroom that is guided by **democratic practice**.

It is likely that each teacher, school, and/or district will also encourage one or more of the following approaches to management. In some cases, management is thought of as discipline. This may be a term used more frequently after an event or a problem; teachers and administrators sometimes use the terms *discipline* and *classroom management* interchangeably. Try to be precise in determining if your rules are those that represent how your classroom is expected to behave, or if you are describing an outcome of behavior.

Citizenship

Citizenship is often thought of as participation or involvement in creating the rules of society. However, other notions of being a citizen also incur the meaning of responsibility. Students who participate must also be responsible for how they participate. One definition, an outcome of a local school district's work on core values in the classroom curriculum, defined citizenship as:

> *The duties, rights, and privileges of the status of citizenship; a person's conduct as a citizen.*

Tempe Union High School District, Tempe, Arizona 1996

Teachers who view their classes as small versions of the larger society may want students to also experience participation in a classroom with both the benefit of citizenship (belonging to a democratic society) and responsibility (following rules). To this end, teachers and schools often plan for their student's behavior by creating a common set of rules.

Planning for a **democratic school community** follows the principles of:

➤ Securing **the public good** (in this case, what is best for the whole class?)
➤ Securing **individual rights**
➤ Determining with and or for the class **what is just and what is fair**
➤ Creating an environment for participation in a society as a citizen of **equal membership** and status.

LF, JF, and **EEO** can guide the discussion and review of citizenship and classroom management.

Strategies for Promoting Citizenship

➤ Build decision making and consequences into your management plan.
➤ Develop class rules around a thematic question such as the responsibilities of a citizen in a school.
➤ Help students learn about participation to the classroom needs (such as helping with resources, cleaning up the room, or cost of materials).
➤ Monitor the use of ethics when working with each other (e.g., do students foster sharing?).
➤ Help students develop respect for one another in their interaction in the room and outside areas of school. Set standards and expectations through discussion and praise.
➤ Ask students to list which rules exist that appear arbitrary, just, fair.
➤ Teach students to vote and abide by a vote.

(*Core Values in the Classroom* 1996 Tempe Union
High School District, Tempe, Arizona)

Consequences

Democratic societies create rules for self-governance and then determine the consequences for these rules. In a **representative democracy (a republic)** an elected official is given the responsibility to create rules (laws) and to enforce these laws with consequences. Thus, the society itself governs, and the laws represent the **values of the society**.

In classrooms, students can learn to develop basic awareness of expectations of the larger society by experiencing **outcomes or consequences of behavior**. Various ways of creating consequences for behavior have been evaluated through research and teacher analysis. Many of the types of consequences that were once used in schools have been deemed unlawful (e.g., spanking or hitting students), and others have replaced such methods with consequences that teach students to think about and integrate the behaviors of responsibility. Some of these strategies that focus on consequences and responsibility appear in this text, and others can be found in additional texts that discuss classroom management.

In any case, the notions of democracy still ask for reflection on **LF, JF**, and **EEO**, and in so doing we as educational leaders analyze our system of what is fair.

Consider several examples of consequences, discussed in-depth in the text *School and Society,* Feinberg and Soltis (1992). These descriptors of application of consequences are called **independence, universalism, specificity**, and **particularity** (p. 19).

Soltis (p.19) describes these terms in the following manner:

➤ **Independence** — responsibility for one's own actions
➤ **Universalism** — a norm of treating all persons with a **standardized basis** of comparison
➤ **Specificity** — exceptions to a rule for a **normed or allowable reason** such as illness
➤ **Particularity** — exception to a rule for an **illegitimate reason** such the student is the child of a fellow teacher

Think of the themes of **LF, JF**, and **EEO** as you review various strategies for consequences.

Strategies for Consequences

- ➢ Ask students if they understand the consequences.
- ➢ Ask students to set their own consequences.
- ➢ Ask students to select one of several consequences.
- ➢ Involve parents in determining consequences.
- ➢ Brainstorm with grade level, department faculty, or administration to determine consequences.
- ➢ Send home a newsletter with rules and consequences for parents to sign.
- ➢ Use pre-consequence warnings such as writing checkmarks on the board, moving a marker across a board, etc.
- ➢ Use community circles or class discussion to set up rules and consequences.
- ➢ Use a chart to show overall class improvement (not individual improvement) in following rules.

Social expectations of how consequences will be created and enforced influence how teachers think about what is fair. Sometimes teachers think that classroom management is only involved in the theories of **independence** (personal responsibility) or **universalism** (standardized application of rules). However, the notions of fairness and justness complicate this application and, thus, it is important to reflect on democratic practice of management strategies.

Think about some of the approaches to classroom management you have read about. Authors of these management plans have suggested many strategies and guidelines for use. Even with good intentions and a plan for positive management, the issues of fairness and equality must be determined.

Some of the management plans below have excellent ideas. Think about how you observe these suggestions in classrooms and how you want to implement some or all of the ideas.

- ➢ Skinner — change behavior through behavior modification
- ➢ Canter — assertive discipline-rewards/punishments
- ➢ Jones —incentives for student self control and responsibility
- ➢ Glasser — choice and personal decision-making
- ➢ Gordon — non-critical with emphasis on conflict resolution and responsibility

(Stamm and Wactler, 1997)

Teacher as Leader for Classroom Management

In a democratic classroom, the teacher usually has thought about many decisions regarding approaches to classroom organization. When making these decisions, the input of those in the constituency, or the populace involved, needs to have representation. The role of the teacher, then, is elected (by virtue of having been given a teaching job as a public trust) and must responsibly represent all constituencies equally. What type of classroom management is most important to your constituencies? Are the parents of your community highly involved with the way school rules are determined or the way consequences are implemented? Read the following case study to decide how you would handle this school scenario:

A parent is very unhappy that her son was kicked during a game played on the yard at recess. This student had kicked another child but had immediately apologized to that student, stating that he was sorry and that it was a mistake. The other student kicked him back anyway. The parent has informed the teacher that school rules should punish the second student for acting out after an apology was given. Further, she stated that, if the school did not implement her rule or punish through consequence, she would encourage her own son to hit back and disregard school rules.

It appears that the parent feels that rules and consequences should not be applied in a system of particularity—in other words, without regard for equal application.

> ➢ What would you do? What rules do you think apply?
> ➢ How would you respond to the parent?
> ➢ What should happen to boy #1? What about boy #2?
> ➢ What is the responsible potential for **citizenship** in this case?
> ➢ What are the possible outcomes to a **democratic** society?

Reflect on the role of the teacher as **democratic educational leader.**

Notes

Classroom Environment Observation Form

Focus on elements of LF, JF, and EEO.

Seating Arrangements

Grouping Students

Diversity in Grouping

Centers for Exploring and Creating

Centers for Direct Instruction

Democratic Practice Reflection

Observation of Classroom Management Form

Focus on elements of LF, JF, and EEO.

Classroom Rules

School Rules

District Rules

Citizenship

Consequences

Teacher as Democratic Leader for Classroom Management

Democratic Practice Reflection

Applying Learning: Activities for Practice

Worksheets

Worksheets are prepared in several styles and formats and are often commercially prepared to follow a textbook. Worksheets give the student an opportunity to practice a skill or to extend his/her learning. Teachers also prepare their own worksheets. Worksheets should contain several elements to be useful for application of learning. The conditions under which worksheets are used vary with the teacher's objective. Sometimes they are used in a timed test, sometimes collaboratively in a group, sometimes as follow-up work to a skills-based lesson such as reading, and other times as seat work or homework. Each teacher decides how and when he/she wants to use worksheets.

> Various themes in **LF**, **JF**, and **EEO** can be seen in the design and use of worksheets for practice.

Strategies for Evaluating Worksheets

Sheets must contain

➢ Clear directions to the student
➢ Information that has recently been taught
➢ Substantial white space for visual clarity
➢ Consistency in lettering size and style and shape
➢ Proper spelling and vocabulary appropriate to grade level and skills taught
➢ A place for student self-identification (name or ID number, period section or hour, grade room number)
➢ Various forms of learning techniques (multiple choice, problem solving, and essay)

Books, Tests, Reports, and Text Materials

When teachers select books for their classrooms, they usually have had some guidance in the way they select these materials. For example, organizations such as the American Library Association have suggested book lists for schools by grade level. School and district curriculum administrators and school curriculum committees have guidelines for book selection. Teachers also have taken university coursework on evaluating good books for students. The criteria for good books are related to the students' grade and age as well as the evidence of literacy value. The local school community and parents will also help schools determine their values in criteria for book selection. Freedom of speech (First Amendment) rights have often been cited as the reason that schools hesitate to banish books from schools. However, the issue is complex and needs serious consideration.

Educational leadership requires that teachers be prepared to help select appropriate reading material and be able to respond to the concerns of all constituencies involved with book selection. Stories that support character education have been long sought after and traditionally supported.

> **Democratic Practice**: Reflect on the elements of **LF, JF**, and **EEO** when considering the importance of textbooks and text materials in your curriculum. For example, some critics report that textbooks can be determinist (influence what is taught), use the lowest common denominator (not challenging), lack opportunity for higher-order thinking skills, present incorrect content, and are written in a formula model (lack creative and innovative use of language).
>
> (Morrison, 1993)

Another theme in the selection of books for students is civics education. Morrison (1993) provides a definition of civics education as reported by the Carnegie Foundation for the Advancement of Teaching (President Ernest L. Boyer).

The ability to participate as a citizen in a democracy concerns the following:

Characteristics of Civics Education

- ➢ Communication *(discourse)*
- ➢ **Action in citizenship**
- ➢ Core knowledge of social issues and institutions of democracy
- ➢ Deal thoughtfully with differences
- ➢ Understanding of how the school works and be allowed to participate and make decisions
- ➢ Connections between what students learn and how they live

(Boyer, 1990, pp. 4-7)

> Reflect on the elements of **LF, JF,** and **EEO** in education for citizenship.

Strategies for Selecting Books

➢ Student grade and age
➢ Goals of the district and the school
➢ Student ability with
  ◆ Content
  ◆ Reading ability
  ◆ Life experience and global perspectives
  ◆ Social skills
➢ Goals for promoting discourse in democracy
➢ Knowledge of social issues and institutions
➢ Goals for promoting action and participation in citizenship
➢ Promotion of higher order thinking
➢ Education for connecting what is learned with how one lives

Tests

Tests are one tool for reporting learning. They can be designed to involve students in their own learning.

➢ Determine **which** curriculum objectives have been taught.
➢ Determine if you want **to measure** the objective(s) taught.
➢ Determine the form of measurement that best represents a true measure of student ability.
➢ Evaluate skills such as student writing ability.

Review the elements of test construction through the elements of **democratic practice**, where on the test **LF**, **JF**, or **EEO** exists.

First determine if the test matches the objectives taught. Is the test designed to be formative (some learning) or summative (all learning)? What is the purpose of the test (student feedback for additional learning, measurement of learning)? Under which circumstances is it best to create a test with multiple choice questions? essay? fill in the blanks? These tools for evaluation have embedded goals of both measurement and feedback.

Strategies for Creating and Using Tests

- ➢ Determine **which** curriculum objectives have been taught.
- ➢ Determine if you want **to measure** the objective(s) taught.
- ➢ Determine the form of measurement that best represents a true measure of student ability.
- ➢ Evaluate skills such as student writing ability.

Reports and Text Material

Another form of applying learning is to write a narrative report (or critique), a summary, a book report, or any variant in prose such as a poem, short story, or myth. This type of writing can be very powerful to a student in applying knowledge and helpful for the teacher in measuring what a student has learned. A key element of this type of writing is to create a rubric or set of standards by which the piece will be judged. For example, if students have learned about the element of meter in writing a poem and now use a poem to tell about a concept in literature, they will need to incorporate this skill in using meter in a poem.

Notice how text material is used in **democratic practice**. Observe elements of **LF**, **JF**, and **EEO** in making decisions about the text material.

Strategies for Reports and Text Material

- ➢ Review the study skills (writing, vocabulary level) needed to complete the report style.
- ➢ Determine which students need another version or a compatible version of the text.
- ➢ Select a text type (report, poem).
- ➢ Let students select their own text type.
- ➢ Set up a rubric for evaluating the text.
- ➢ Let students create their own rubric for evaluation.
- ➢ Determine the evaluative weight of the text (points, extra credit).
- ➢ Display the text (bulletin boards, newsletters, books).
- ➢ Create a permanent binding or a portfolio of text.
- ➢ Submit text material for contests and scholarships.
- ➢ Involve community experts (e.g. local journalists, writers, poets) in creating and supporting text material.
- ➢ Invite parents and community members to help students create text.
- ➢ Showcase reports and text with a poem reading, literature study, or book review.
- ➢ Create or support a book club on campus.

Notes

Technology and Other Applied Projects

The proliferation of computers and support technology in schools has allowed many teachers to develop new approaches to curriculum development. In part, this development means that curriculum is designed with both teachers and students searching for and analyzing information for their classes (Stamm and Wactler, 1997). The use of technology has opened up not only a global perspective of information but also an additional perspective on approaches to the value of information (Doll, 1993; Slattery, 1995; Stamm and Wactler, 1997). It is no wonder that teachers today use software such as Internet search engines to find information prior to creating lessons.

In writing about the moral dilemma of teaching, Stamm and Wactler (1997) and Wactler (1997) have proposed that the role of the teacher shifts slightly in the post-modern era of vast information access. For example, computer accessibility may also mean that teachers now have to help students create the moral filters of responsible use of information. Stamm and Wactler term this role of the teacher **the Informationist** and contend that, as such, the teacher helps students use strategies of higher-order thinking when they analyze the best use of information.[*]

Various formats for computer use and curriculum development have been suggested. For example, the use of the CD-ROM **Math*ed*ology Program** can increase both the math skills of teachers and their ability to teach mathematics (Bitter and Pryor, 1996). Teachers' use of this CD-ROM program has also been found to increase skill in the use of planning for discourse for

---

[*] For more information on the role of the teacher, see Part Three, Chapter Four.

democracy in the classroom (Wactler, 1998). Schools use and organize computers in many ways. Students often use computers for practicing skills in language, writing, and math programs (see Tempe Unified School District, Tempe, Arizona). Finally, students use computers in various formats (e.g., in pairs as they support each other as partners, a content search as well as skill in the use of the computer, or independently for similar purposes).

For some schools, computers are available in every classroom, sometimes with several in each classroom (see Plano, Texas School System). Other districts have given each teacher in the district their own laptop computer for home and school use (see Kyrene School District, Tempe, Arizona). The notion that computers are key to future skill development and a wide base of content information has in part guided the wide use of computers in schools. Some districts, however, have little funding for computers and have had corporate partners supply computers to schools. Finally, it is not unknown to find schools without computers at all, even in the library! These schools find that parents and the community desire computers, but funding has not been available.

> Review issues of **LF**, **JF**, and **EEO** as you observe the use of computers in schools.

Strategies for Computer Use

- ➤ Operational computer skills
- ➤ On-line library search
- ➤ Report writing
- ➤ Skills (language, math) practice
- ➤ Content search
- ➤ E-mail and other types of communication
- ➤ Graphic design
- ➤ Accounting and principles of statistics
- ➤ Independent use of computers
- ➤ Teacher/student collaboration
- ➤ Teacher-led use of computers
- ➤ Student/student use of computers
- ➤ Community-led (engineers and programmer experts) use of computers

Notes

Multi-Media, Tapes, Video and Photos

Teachers use various types of media in their classrooms. Not unlike the book selection process, some of these media require a district or school (even a department chair) review. Videotapes used by teachers are typically pre-approved by curriculum teams consisting of parents, community members, administrators, and teachers. Tapes such as music also are reviewed for content and appropriateness for age/grade.

The most common medium used by teachers is photographs. Magazines, commercial pictures, and personal pictures are found in most classrooms. Sometimes students themselves bring in photos for display in the classroom.

Another form of medium is slogans and banners. Schools have used banners for motivation, and such banners often proclaim the school's slogan or mission statement. However, other types of banners may appear controversial, and these banners have had communities divided about their use. For example, banners regarding moral behavior such as the use of drugs or reminders about various forms of sex education have met with various responses both in and out of schools.

Some teachers feel that no form of censorship should be enforced if the media used support an academic objective. Other constituents (such as parents or administrators) worry that a misrepresentation of values could occur and feel that a filter for media (even newspapers) is needed.

In thinking about the use of media in the classroom, reflect on elements of **LF**, **JF**, and **EEO**.

Strategies for Using Multi-Media

➤ Create a center for the use of media (such as a media table for tapes).
➤ Involve all constituents in the evaluation of media.
➤ Create a rubric for the use of media (such as the use of a video for biography).
➤ Focus on the stated objective in achievement.
➤ Use a concrete form to support the use of media (e.g., a handout to guide the viewing of a video).
➤ State the expected objective outcomes to the class.
➤ Decide if some type of evaluation of student learning is needed after the use of media.
➤ Update your use of media and review district approval lists.
➤ Find materials that are unique or expand the students' experiences.

Homework and Projects Due

Another form of applying learning is homework assignments and a variety of short- to long-term projects. Some project, such as trying to find materials to surround an egg that is dropped from the height of a building (and that supports the egg without smashing it) are fun and informative for high school physics classes! Other projects such as routine practice of math problems sometimes do not feel like fun or even appear to interest students. Teachers often complain that homework is not completed or, if it is completed, is not given much effort. One way to alleviate problems with homework is to use the progressive approach of John Dewey (1859-1952) and ask students what forms of practice in homework they enjoy most.

Students can be very creative about practice. They may want to demonstrate their ability to recite poetry by creating a video and showing their tape to the class. They may want to write their own newsletter and inform the class of their ability to write newsworthy stories!

Sometimes students do not complete homework. They can be involved in many after-school activities and think that they can make up their requirements. Homework policies and makeup work are often an area of confrontation and conflict between teachers and students and their parents. Be certain to review the policies for homework and determine that they are well grounded, fair, and just.

Some consideration should be given to **how** homework/projects will be completed. Will the students be expected to work alone? In pairs or small groups? How will you grade this work? Should all homework and projects be graded? Will resources be available?

> Review elements of **LF**, **JF**, and **EEO** as you observe homework and project policies.

Strategies for Homework and Projects

➤ Create a homework policy.
➤ Ask students for feedback about the policy.
➤ Determine if and how grades will be given (can students self-evaluate/correct?).
➤ Vary the type of homework.
➤ Vary the work pattern for students (some pairs, some individual).
➤ If graded, return homework as soon as possible.
➤ Collaborate in person and on the Internet with other teachers for homework ideas.
➤ Supply resources for homework and projects (Internet, library reserve).

Observation of Worksheets Form

Focus on elements of LF, JF, and EEO.

Directions

Worksheet Link to Objective Taught

Variety in Learning (Multiple Choice, Essay, and Problem Solving)

Variety in Worksheet Use (Independent, Peer, or Group)

Meets Needs of Learners at Various Levels of Understanding

Democratic Practice Reflection

Observation of Books Form

Focus on elements of LF, JF, and EEO.

Student Grade and Age

District and School Goals

Student Ability Level (Content, Reading, Life and Global Experience, Social Skills)

Knowledge of Social Issues and Institutions

Promotion of Action and Participation in Citizenship

Promotion of Higher Order Thinking

Connection of What is Learned to How One Lives

Democratic Practice Reflection

Observation of Tests Form

Focus on elements of LF, JF, and EEO.

Which curriculum objectives have been taught?

Will the objective(s) be measured?

What type of measurement is used?

Evaluate students' skill level.

Alternative or extended testing? (extra credit?)

Democratic Practice Reflection

Observation of Reports and Text Material Form

Focus on elements of LF, JF, and EEO.

What are the study skills needed to complete the report?

Is a compatible version of text style needed?

Who selected text style?

How was rubric determined?

What is the type (if any) of evaluation of text?

What types of permanent display of text are used (contests, binding, or portfolio)?

What community resources are used in creating text?

What type of parental/community involvement is involved in creating text?

What type of showcase is used for text material (display board, newsletter)?

Are other activities involved in creating text (campus club)?

Democratic Practice Reflection

Observation of Books for Civics Education Form

Focus on elements of LF, JF, and EEO.

Describe the elements of discourse (communication) in the book.

What elements for action in citizenship are found in the book?

What core knowledge of social issues and institutions of democracy are discussed?

Does the book foster decision making?

Does the book help make connections between what students learn and how they live?

Democratic Practice Reflection

Observation of Technology Use Form

Focus on elements of LF, JF, and EEO

What type of technology will be used? Describe computer, software, CD-ROM, ancillary materials.

What type of computer skills will be needed (word processing, graphics, spreadsheets)?

What is the objective for use (on-line library search, report, content, multiple uses)?

How will the technology be organized for use (individual, pairs, groups, several ways)?

Who will guide the use of technology (teacher, student, visitor)?

Democratic Practice Reflection

Observation of Multi-Media, Tapes, Video and Photos

Focus on elements of LF, JF, and EEO.

How is the medium organized (table, center, independent)?

Who helped evaluate this medium (parents, students, teacher)?

Is there a rubric for the use of the medium?

Are there materials to guide the use of the medium (e.g., a handout)?

What form of medium evaluation is used?

Do the materials used expand the students' experiences (such as use of classical music)?

Has the medium been reviewed by district, school, department, or grade level?

Democratic Practice Reflection

Observation of Homework and Projects Due Form

Focus on elements of LF, JF, and EEO.

What is the homework policy?

Who created the policy (students, parents, administration, and/or teacher)?

What is the grading policy for the homework or project?

Does the homework or project type vary?

Does the work pattern for students vary (pairs, individual, and groups)?

When and how are grades returned?

Has there been collaboration about homework (other teachers, Internet)?

What resources do students have for completing homework or projects (homework hot line, Internet)?

Democratic Practice Reflection

Evaluation and Grading

Grading on a Bell Curve

Many projects, tests, papers, and even speeches are given a point value as feedback and evaluation of attainment. Students have spent many years receiving a specified number of points for the work that they do. Grounded in the **executive** or production model of teaching, this type of point system allows a teacher to use a rubric and grade work efficiently (Soltis, 1992; Stamm and Wactler, 1997). However, once a student receives the assigned points, the grade impact may have new implications.

Grading on a bell curve is a form of grading where the average score of the class is re-adjusted so that the curve or middle score reflects the scores of the class as a whole. If, for example, you have determined that the grade of *C* is attained at the lowest level by a score of 70, and the entire class does not do well on a test, using a bell curve would allow you to consider the entire class's attainment and to readjust the curve to represent the middle. Thus, a poorly achieving class could then find that a score of 60 is now a grade of *C*.

In reviewing the policy of grading on a curve, or "the bell curve," a teacher considers several aspects of grading.

Consider various elements of **LF**, **JF**, and **EEO** when using the bell curve for evaluation.

Strategies for Grading on a Bell Curve

➢ Consider the students' abilities to perform on the test or project (reading level, math level).
➢ Review the test questions for internal validity (were some questions too hard? too easy?).
➢ Review the methods used for testing (clear directions, familiar test type).
➢ Consider the conditions of testing (before lunch, after a rainstorm or a school prom).
➢ Consider the class's previous experience with test taking.
➢ Review your own teaching (did you teach to the objective? did you cover all the material?).

Using a Percentage Grading Scale

Similar to the bell curve, a percentage grading scale uses a point system for evaluation. However, the percentage grading scale is based on the mastery of objectives at a fixed level of expertise, regardless of class attainment. Thus, a predetermined rubric with points per item and a fixed scale are the tools a teacher uses in this evaluation system. For example, if a teacher devises a percentage scale for 100 percent, then a point score of 90 would receive a grade of *A,* 80 points a grade of *B,* etc. If all members of the class score a 90, then all students receive a grade of "*A.*"

Consider elements of **LF**, **JF**, and **EEO** when using a percentage grading scale.

Strategies for Grading with a Percentage Grading Scale

➢ Consider the objectives to be mastered and the proficiency level for each level of mastery.

➢ Review past classes, grade level/department and district objectives and align proficiency for mastery.

➢ Consider the evaluation tools and their impact (such as reading ability) on mastery.

➢ Review your teaching and be certain all objectives were taught.

➢ Consider the conditions for teaching and testing (e.g., was the school under construction?).

➢ Are you new to the grade/department?

➢ Were resources available for students?

Affective Evaluation: Creativity, Effort, and Resources

When reviewing the efforts of students, teachers often consider how hard students have worked on a project, how innovative and creative they have been, or what types of new or thoughtful resources they have used in a project or test.

For example, a well-written essay that uses references from a broad base of literature and historical data may be more highly rated than a more thinly described effort, even though they both answer the question correctly! How will you account for this difference? Will you account for a difference?

Another example is the innovative use of resources. Sometimes a student uses old resources such as art or science materials and creates an interesting perspective on a topic. This is often viewed in students' work in preparation for science fairs. Will you consider the way in which resources were used when you grade? How will you do this?

Finally, there is creativity, a subjective topic, yet one that is often ignored in a world of executive grading and attainment. When a student re-thinks what he/she has learned and demonstrates a creative answer, how important will this type of thought be when you consider grading?

Consider the elements of **LF**, **JF**, and **EEO** when you grade for affective effort.

Strategies for Affective Evaluation

➢ Determine if the student's effort, innovation, and creativity are unique and exhibited well.

➢ Have thoughtful or creative resources been used?

➢ Have resources been used in a unique manner?

➢ Has the student demonstrated higher-order thinking or strategies of synthesis?

Evaluating Improvement

Students gain mastery of subjects in a variety of ways. Some demonstrate their mastery on tests and papers, while others demonstrate this mastery in verbal feedback or class discussions. In either case, it is important to notice how and when a student's performance is improving. In grading improvement, a teacher should consider the effect of the attention to improvement on the student's sense of self and future attainment. For example, when a second grader starts to spell more words correctly each week, but the average score does not increase enough to raise a grade, should you consider effort and improvement in grading? If a high school English student, who has never memorized Shakespeare, now recites a sonnet in a beautiful and compassionate manner, should you consider this attempt and new venture as part of his/her grade? Teachers vary in their responses.

Consider the elements of **LF**, **JF**, and **EEO** when you evaluate improvement.

Strategies for Evaluating Improvement

➢ Consider each student's abilities.
➢ Consider using improvement as only part of a grade.
➢ Consider separating grades for attainment from grades for improvement.
➢ Use improvement as extra credit.
➢ Review your teaching and notice if you have changed your strategies to support student learning.

Notes

Portfolio Grading

Portfolios are collections of student materials. The collection can contain items such as essays, reports, tests, and quizzes, and even sample homework assignments. Some teachers use a rubric and pre-determine what should be placed in a portfolio. Others simply ask students to put their best or favorite work into their portfolios. Portfolios are a good way to demonstrate attainment and improvement of ability. They can also show student interest in a topic such as baseball or cars. Artwork is often found in portfolios. When grading the portfolio, be certain to ascertain which type of collection method you used and discuss the evaluation of the portfolio with each student. You could choose to ask students to self-grade some of their work.

Use the elements of **LF**, **JF**, and **EEO** when grading portfolios.

Strategies for Grading Portfolios

➢ Create a rubric for types of materials to include and grading policy.
➢ Let students decide on the materials to include and how to grade them.
➢ Collaborate with students on both materials and grading policy.
➢ Vary the types of materials included.
➢ Change the materials in the portfolio often.
➢ Showcase the portfolios at open house/parents night.
➢ Have students show and teach other classes how to create a portfolio.

Age/Grade and Content Alignment

School districts create a scope and sequence of curriculum as a guideline for teachers to align with their classroom teaching. This scope and sequence describes what the grade/age curriculum for each subject should be. Usually, the districts have aligned this curriculum with the state board of education goals for students. This alignment also covers the sequence, or teaching order, of the curriculum. For example, in math, second graders learn about addition and its opposite, subtraction. Which do you teach first? The scope and sequence of a district curriculum shows how to align your teaching with the prepared goals of the school district. This document also describes content as appropriate for a grade level. The community and parents are informed of this information.

What if you want to change the age/grade/content alignment?

When you evaluate your students' progress, it is important to consider district goals. A curriculum committee of parents, community, teachers, and administrators has determined these goals. If you grade your students on material that is not age/grade- or content-appropriate, you must consider all elements of **LF**, **JF**, and **EEO**. For example, suppose you would like to teach a unit about United States history to your fourth graders. Typically, this unit is taught in the fifth grade. What aspects of grading are you able to use that allow for grading that is **fair and just**? Are your students prepared for this unit? What skills will they need (reading level, conceptual understanding, higher-order thinking)? Is it fair that you cannot teach and grade without consideration of district and state goals?

Consider elements of **LF**, **JF**, and **EEO** when you grade for age/grade and content alignment.

Strategies for Age/Grade and Content Alignment

➤ Review scope and sequence of school district curriculum goals.
➤ Meet with grade level/department for alignment.
➤ Review the skills, abilities, and conceptual understanding of your students.
➤ Review and monitor students' interests.

Narrative Evaluation

Written or oral narratives are also used as methods of determining achievement. Students' responses during discussion, short responses in small groups, and formal oral and written reports are ways that students can demonstrate mastery of content and innovation in description of the content.

When determining a grade for class participation, take into account the previously discussed section on improvement. Think about how difficult it may be to develop speaking skills. Think about how you use questioning strategies to support the ability of all to participate. Have your strategies implemented equal opportunity for everyone to speak?

Written narrative is often a product formed from a rubric. One example is the written book report and analysis of a book. Another example is a creative poem or even a song. How will you grade this type of product?

Review the elements of **LF**, **JF**, and **EEO** as you observe methods of narrative evaluation.

Strategies for Narrative Evaluation

➤ Review your questioning strategies for implementation of higher-order thinking.
➤ Analyze your strategies to provide an opportunity for everyone to participate.
➤ Determine what elements of creativity are important to grade and how to grade them.
➤ Consider the students' effort such as public speaking.
➤ Consider the students' improvement such as faster response or a more descriptive answer.
➤ Set up a rubric for content analysis in evaluation such as the demonstration of clear writing or the use of a type of writing.
➤ Think about how small groups are balanced (e.g., will everyone will have an opportunity to speak?).

The Extra-Credit/Mastery Model

When teachers provide for extra credit (for example, a test or homework), they expect that the student will be extending current learning to a higher level. Sometimes, extra credit is simply extra practice. In either case, the teacher offers extra points for completing the work correctly. Usually a time limit is set on when the work can be completed. Sometimes students who do not get a score that they wanted will ask for an opportunity for extra work to achieve extra credit. For example, if a student scores a 79 on a test (typically a grade of *C*), this student may want to do some extra credit work to improve his/her grade and receive a grade of *B*.

Since the student who reached a *B* did so during the first test or paper turned in, is it democratic (fair or just) to allow another student to add to his/her score? Or, as in the **mastery model**, is the goal simply to demonstrate mastery, and therefore the number of times it takes to reach this score is not important?

In the **mastery model**, students may take a test over and over again and stop when they feel they have mastered the content and received the grade they wanted. Do you think this is wise? Is it democratic?

Review the elements of **LF**, **JF**, and **EEO** as you observe methods of extra-credit/mastery learning in evaluation.

Notes

Observation of Grading on a Bell Curve or a Percentage Grading Scale Form

Focus on elements of LF, JF, and EEO.

What type of grading format was used (bell curve or percentage grading scale)?

What was the students' content ability (reading, math)?

What testing methods were used (test type)?

What were the testing conditions?

Had the class taken many tests before? of this type?

Did you teach to the objective?

Did you review department/grade level content and align for mastery?

What resources were available to students?

Democratic Practice Reflection

Observation of Creativity, Effort/Improvement, and Resources in Evaluation

Focus on elements of LF, JF, and EEO.

Describe the student effort, innovation, and creativity level.

Were resources (essay, poem) used in a thoughtful or unique manner?

Was there a demonstration of higher order thinking or strategies of synthesis?

What consideration should there be for each student's abilities?

Have you used new strategies to support student learning?

Consider the placement of the improvement grade (part of grade, separate from attainment, extra credit)?

Democratic Practice Reflection

Observation of Portfolio Evaluation Form

Focus on elements of LF, JF, and EEO.

Describe the rubric for the portfolio.

Did the students have input in the portfolio design?

Are the materials representative of the objectives taught?

What type of grading rubric has been developed?

How have the materials been showcased or displayed?

Have the students shared their portfolios with others?

Democratic Practice Reflection

Observation of Age/Grade and Content Alignment Form

Focus on elements of LF, JF, and EEO.

List the state standards for age/grade.

Describe the scope and sequence of school district age/grade goals.

What alignment outcomes were determined by the grade level of department?

What are the skills, abilities, and conceptual attainment of students?

What additional understanding do you have of the students?

What are the students' interests?

Democratic Practice Reflection

Observation of Narrative Evaluation Form

Focus on elements of LF, JF, and EEO.

Describe the questioning strategies for implementation of higher-order thinking.

Analyze strategies to provide opportunity for all to participate.

Determine which elements of creativity are important to evaluate and how to grade them.

Consider student effort (such as public speaking).

Consider student improvement (faster response, more descriptive answer).

Set up a rubric for content analysis in evaluation (clear writing, use of a specific style of writing).

How are small groups balanced so that everyone has an opportunity to participate?

Democratic Practice Reflection

Observation of Extra-Credit/Mastery Model Form

Focus on elements of LF, JF, and EEO.

Is extra credit offered for extension of learning? Describe.

Is extra credit offered for practice of learning? Describe.

How is extra credit graded? Describe.

Is extra credit offered to improve an overall grade or a grade on a test or project?

What is the policy for extra credit? Do all students have this opportunity? Under what circumstances?

Should students be offered the opportunity to demonstrate mastery with multiple opportunities (such as multiple test taking)?

Democratic Practice Reflection

Special Education

Special needs students usually have some type of need that requires a special program or service. These types of programs may be available in your school district: programs for children with physical, linguistic, hearing, visual, mental, or learning disabilities and children with special giftedness or talents. Other considerations of special needs are the understanding that children come to school with many types of at-risk factors in their lives, social and personal needs among them. Needs such as safe or adequate homes may be factors in the children's lives, and these needs require the teacher to assess the school/community social environment.

Meeting student needs is found in the work of Abraham Maslow and is key to a humanist approach to teaching (Enz, Cook, and Matani, 1998; Morrison, 1993; Stamm and Wactler, 1997; and Soltis, 1992). Maslow believed that the goal of education is self-actualization and that human needs must be satisfied before those of a higher order such as academic attainment (Morrison, 1993).

Students with disabilities are termed by the federal government as handicapped children, and those so identified have met the following requirement:

> *...those children evaluated...as being mentally retarded, hard of hearing, deaf, speech impaired, visually handicapped, seriously emotionally disturbed, orthopedically impaired, other health impaired, deaf-blind, multi-handicapped or as having specific learning disabilities, who because of those impairments need special education and related services.*
> (*Federal Register*, Aug. 23, 1977, p. 42, 478)

The most well known guideline to federal law regarding special needs children is Public Law 94-142, which includes provisions for a free and appropriate education for all persons between ages 3 and 21, in an environment that is least restrictive for learning best. The Individual Education Plan (IEP) is a document created for planning for a handicapped student's instruction and must consider all conditions relevant to this student's needs. The parents of the handicapped child have many rights extended to them so they can participate in developing, with the school district, a plan that is appropriate for their child.

One method used by school districts to support special needs of children is a format called **mainstreaming**. This process allows for social and educational integration of special needs children into the general instruction or regular class process (Morrison, 1993). Usually, this means that the special needs child will be in the regular classroom for all or part of the day (when appropriate) and at times with a resource teacher. At times, the resource teacher or support teacher will be in the regular classroom with the child. Another form of schooling is for the child to work with the resource teacher outside of the regular classroom. When a child works outside the regular classroom, the program is termed "a pull-out program." This is often the case with children with special language needs.

Consider the elements of **LF**, **JF**, and **EEO** in reflecting on special needs students.

Strategies for Special Needs Students

➤ Review the models of student placement (such as mainstreaming, use of aides, school wide support, and use of support centers [usually for secondary education]).

➤ Vary the presentation, pace, and types of assignments.

➤ Use various devices and materials to support the student.

➤ Use forms of student support such as a peer buddy or tutors.

➤ Adapt the environment to the student (chair and table heights).

(Glass, 1977)

Gifted Programs

Gifted students have been identified through programs that test for intellectual ability. Talented students are those with special gifts in areas such as music or sports (Morrison, 1993). Researchers such as Joseph S. Renzulli report that there are three components to the definition of giftedness: above average intelligence, task commitment, and creativity (Morrison, 1993). Morrison reports that Renzulli developed an enrichment model for curriculum development that sequences the following steps:

➤ The acquainting of students with various activities

➤ Group activities that promote thinking and feeling

➤ Activities that investigate real problems

(Morrison, 1993)

The gifted student, like the special needs handicapped student, is usually mainstreamed into the regular classroom. Morrison (1993) writes that there is a tendency to provide special classes for gifted students in order to be inclusive; however, many regular classroom teachers can and do provide enrichment and accelerated work. In high schools, the content classifications (such as advanced placement courses) often offer this type of accelerated work. Sources that can be used in the elementary years to provide support for gifted students can also include resource pull-out teachers, community mentors (such as an engineer), independent work, and special classes or schools (Morrison, 1993). It appears that the resource room, a pull-out room for special support, is the most popular.

> Reflect on elements of **LF**, **JF**, and **EEO** in considering gifted students.

Strategies for Gifted Students

> ➤ Vary the curriculum.
> ➤ Select materials and resources that can be used in a creative manner.
> ➤ Try to extend the regular projects into a related field (such as aviation history in a regular history class).
> ➤ Encourage the student to pursue special or personal interests.
> ➤ Use community resource persons.
> ➤ Become aware of the resource room materials and teacher's curriculum.

Language Acquisition Programs

Many students enrolled in schools today are from many parts of the world and come to school with various language abilities. Some speak their first language entirely; others have learned some English. Others have no skills in their own language.

The debate regarding the efficacy of special needs language programs such as English as a second language, bilingual, or even dual language programs appear to rest on issues of linguistic, social, cultural, political and economic perspectives as well those issues that are strictly educational (Oliva, 1992). Thus, the opportunities and resources for various language programs can vary from community to community. The U.S. Supreme Court case of *Lau v Nichols* required San Francisco to provide English education for Chinese-speaking students (Oliva, 1993). The issue of how a student learns best, however, is not entirely a debate regarding language acquisition skills.

Oliva (1992) writes that "the opposing philosophies of acculturation versus pluralism remains as a focus of this type of discussion" (p. 537). Various forms of bilingual or bicultural class constructs are used. Sometimes the students are mainstreamed into the regular classroom, and at other times they are in the regular classroom, with pull-out for language acquisition. In other school settings, students are in a dual language class that contains only non- or limited English speakers. Usually schools that request bilingual funds also must demonstrate some teaching in the native language to support content skills. Oliva (1992) writes that bilingual education remains a sensitive issue.

Writing in support of language acquisition programs, Duane E. Campbell (1996) defines such programs as those that support the:

Acquisition of basic communicative competency in a second language is a function of comprehensible second-language instruction and a supportive environment.

(p. 264)

Campbell suggests support strategies in language acquisition based on the work of Crawford (1989) in the California Case Studies project. The controversy between bilingual instruction over English language development appears to focus on content development. The argument for bilingual education rests on the acquisition of such skills as reading and math in a primary language and as a primary effort. The development of English as a priority rests on the case for rapid development of English skills. Transitional practice is the use of the home language for a few years for content development, with the attainment of English skills in the process (Campbell, 1996).

One form of transition is termed **sheltered English**, or **sheltered instruction**. This instruction uses amplification of the context of language, interactive teaching strategies and dialog, clarification, language simplification, modeling, and cooperative learning (Campbell, 1996, pp. 256-57).

> Reflect on elements of **LF**, **JF**, and **EEO** in considering language programs.

Strategies for Language Acquisition Programs

➤ Use of English as a second language (ESL) and sheltered English instruction in academic content areas
➤ Use of bilingual education for content areas, particularly in grades K-4
➤ Use of schema building, modeling, and frequent clarification
➤ Strong communication and context focus
➤ Interactive teaching
➤ Low-anxiety environment and comprehensible input such as role-playing and pictures

(Campbell, 1996, p. 256-57)

Strategies for Limited English-Proficient Students

➤ Use of native language to teach cognitively demanding subjects, and supplementary materials in the native language

➢ Well-trained teachers to provide instruction in native language
➢ Avoid mixing English and native language during instruction.
➢ Acceptance of regional and nonstandard varieties of the native language

(Campbell, 1996. p. 263-64)

Strategies for Understanding Culture and Language Acquisition

➢ Recognize each culture's value and status.
➢ Include parents and community in conversations about the value of the native language and culture and the learned language and culture.
➢ Encourage bilingualism.
➢ Encourage the development of both cultural systems.
➢ Encourage cross-cultural respect.

(Campbell, 1996, pp. 265-66)

Technology and Computers

George Morrison (1996) cites the perspective of Gary Bitter, president of the International Society for Technology in Education, in describing the relationship between technology and the nation's need for improvement of our educational system:

The United States as a nation must recognize the need for improvement in its educational system and seize the opportunities offered by technology. Technology must be tightly woven into the curriculum, rather than being merely a supplement to the curriculum. (p. 419)

Morrison (1996, p. 419) reports that Bitter's suggestions for the integration of technology into school and education are

➢ Creating a national trust fund to ensure equal access to technology
➢ Empowering teachers through in-service education and supplying them with computers and technology
➢ Ensuring equal access to technology through a commitment for integrating technology into the curricula

> ➤ Strengthening school-industry alliances and forming a national computer communications network
> ➤ Creating effective workplace technologies to streamline the management of schools

In writing about approaches to teaching and the role of the teacher, Stamm and Wactler (1997) described an emerging post-modernist perspective calling for a review of technology in the teacher's philosophical role and to term this approach to teaching the informationist (p. 60).

In this role, the teacher emerges as a leader, but one whose role is rather parallel to that of the student (for more information on the various roles of the teacher, see Part Three, Chapter Four). The teacher guides students to create their own meaning of information and provides a venue for thinking about information. As the students become interested and proficient in finding information, the teacher may reverse roles with the students and become the learner. In this informationist model, students and teachers share both information and the way in which information could be used.

A Case Study

On an Internet search, some students found that students in emerging democratic countries were in need of school supplies. The students asked their teacher if they could take up a schoolwide drive for helping to supply these students with some basic classroom needs, such as dictionaries in their own language, paper supplies and music tapes. The teacher became aware of the students' need for guidance in policy and process and searched for school and government contacts on the Internet. She also searched for district policy and community financial support.

Other uses of the Internet have been to develop curriculum units and lesson plans for these units (C. Wactler, Eruditio Project, Arizona State University 1997-1998). Teachers can find web sites such as Mars, the Red Planet projects, NASA and space exploration, or even the biosphere project. Each of the web sites has multiple uses for classroom teachers. They can find content information. They can look at some pre-structured curriculum units and lesson plans. They can share their own ancillary web sites with other teachers in a chat room and share curriculum development.

One teacher in Tempe, Arizona (Arizona State University/Scales Professional Development School) worked as projected by using recommendations such as those of Gary Bitter in the preceding text. The teacher and students searched the Web together and created their own unit for content. In this case, the students, along with their student teacher and classroom teacher, searched for and found multiple web sites for the Mars project and then created their own science unit. The result was that the entire cohort learned a great deal about content, about how to share information, and about how to use technology. This type of triangulation suggests collaboration for the practice of democracy in the classroom.

Unsolved, however, is the issue of equality in access. Many districts have access vis-à-vis newer schools and buildings prepared for technology. Others have more district or corporate funding for newer technological advances. Some districts are still struggling with getting basic computers with low modem speed.

Consider the following issue presented by one high school student in Texas:

Is Self-interest Democratic, Dad? A Philosophical Response to Education for Justice
Caroline Wactler
Arizona State University

My niece, Ashley, had just entered ninth grade, high school in her Texas suburb. At dinner one evening, she asked her father why her high school could not just give its surplus (?) computers to the neighboring school district. She said, "We have many extra, they never get used, and we have more computers than we need." Her father responded by explaining the processes needed in order to complete such a transaction and replied further that it was unlikely to happen. Teenagers rarely take no easily, and Ashley again asked the obvious, "If we have so many, is it fair that others go without?" Yeah, Ashley. Go for justice. Describe a construct of fairness, but remember, then, that democracy may not feel fair (Wactler, 1997).

If educators answer Ashley by responding that democracy allows for individual success for all, we must address for her all the issues regarding education in a democracy and support a philosophical construct that includes some vision of justice (Strike, 1989). She is waiting for an answer that is fair. And, now we must decide: Is America educating for a democratic society, and if so, is that education fair? To that end, we **all** want to concur somehow that if educating for democracy is NOT fair, then what should a re-configuration look like (Wactler, 1998)?

As Ashley told us, "Well, Dad, why don't we just change things to make them fair?" Leave it to teenagers. Her last statement before dessert was, "Well, if you can't change it, maybe I can." The inference is that maybe we don't want to change. Perhaps America prefers its definition of democracy and has not, in a clear-headed manner, defined for itself what the outcome is for the non-vested part of society (Wactler, 1998).

Reflect on **LF**, **JF**, and **EEO** in thinking about technology and computers.

Strategies for the Use of Technology and Computers

➤ Research the technology available in your district and become familiar with it.

➤ Enlist the help of technology experts in your district.

➤ Take courses or district-sponsored classes in technology.

➤ Learn about curriculum and lesson plan development on the Web.

➤ Search the Web for content and areas of interest to students.

➤ Search the Web with students and develop varied patterns of working (such as pairs, teams).

➤ Vary the type of assignments that can be done on the computer (journals, e-mail, Web searches, reports, computer-assisted library searches).

➤ Find community volunteers and parents who can assist in aspects of the use of technology.

➤ Align course requirements and grading with the use of computer technology.

Media Labs and Libraries

Many schools have designed media centers or labs for computer use. Others have a library section set aside for the use of computers. Media typically are loaded with software that assists students in various tasks. Morrison describes the types of software functions as drill and practice, tutorials, stimulation, and exploratory/game (1993, p. 422). Districts may use software that helps them monitor curriculum development and student progress (Morrison, 1993). Libraries support the use of media or computer labs by cataloging (usually on-line) and housing the texts, software, tapes, and videos that can be adjunct to information derived from a computer. For example, children's literature is collected and housed on bookshelves for students. Often a librarian teaches special lessons for students during 'library time." These lessons for library process may be either lessons such as "How to use the library or media center" or a directed literature lesson. Additionally, students can reserve time with both the computer lab and the library.

In either case, some of the issues regarding **LF, JF,** and **EEO** that affect students regard issues of access and censorship. Similar to issues that in the past were reserved for libraries or classroom textbook selection, information access issues now extend to the computer and searches on the Internet.

A Case Study

Think about how on-line Web services are selected for student use. Does your district buy an Internet service that has filtered the information available to students? Is this supportive of the age/grade
and scope and sequence of district and classroom goals? Does it align with your goals for **LF**, **JF**, and **EEO**? Should students have access to the entire Web of information?

Consider the elements of **LF**, **JF**, and **EEO** when reflecting on issues such as software consideration and access issues.

Strategies for Review of Software

➢ Alignment of curriculum to software
➢ Context alignment of software to student understanding
➢ Accurate content
➢ Students involved in their own learning
➢ Scope and sequence and age-appropriate
➢ Determination if the program is free of technical errors
➢ Comparison of the software with other resources such as texts
➢ Determination if the students can use the software without teacher guidance

(Morrison, 1993, p. 428)

Music, Art, and Physical Education

The Arts

Programs that support the affective way of knowing (Eisner, 1982) have been part of school curriculum tradition. They are programs that allow for expression of a creative part of student development. These programs are usually taught by specialists with training in special areas; however, in many elementary schools, funds and personnel are not available for these teacher specialists. In this case, the regular classroom teacher becomes the artist and the physical education teacher, and learns the rules of many games and how to teach basic play skills to students.

In the case of art and music, university coursework or in-service courses can supplement information for the regular teacher. Districts also have content resources that can be accessed. Furthermore, this area can be supplemented by some community and parental support through clubs and direct involvement in teaching. Community resources such as museum aides and lecturers often bring their personnel right into the classroom.

The area of democratic practice that requires review may be the issues that are curriculum-related. For example, what in the content of art may be considered controversial and why? What types of affective knowing should be reviewed first by districts or administrations? What types of decisions are you prepared and willing to become a leader in or to support?

A Case Study

A junior high school English department decided to show a video of a well-known novel. The novel had been on an approved list of books to read. However, in video form, the graphic representation of the book was (or appeared to be) amplified. The presentation of war and violence caused some students to talk about the video at home. Parents, who had signed consent forms, who had the opportunity to preview the video and take their students out of the class for the day, still protested the video. The teachers in the English department had followed school policy. Should the video be taken off the resource list for the following year? What should the teacher do now that the video has been shown? What should teachers tell students about censure issues? What messages about **LF**, **JF**, and **EEO** are students learning?

Physical Education

Get Active—Be Happy!

Wall and Murray (1990) have defined physical education as an all-encompassing experience that promotes the skill development of the entire child (examples are areas such as dance or games). Physical education programs in public schools have been designed to insure health and education for students. Vogel and Seefeldt (1988) have described a sequence of identifying criteria for performance in health education that supports the development of a physical education program of fitness and skill level. Logsdon, Alleman, Clark, and Sakola (1986) have described types of dance, games, and gymnastics that focus on the developmental phases and stages of child development.

Other related areas of physical education that have evolved into issues regarding fairness and freedom (and equality) are

> ➢ The humanization of physical education (issues such as problem solving, honesty, and fairness) (Burdis, 1987; Kohn, 1986)

> ➤ Health education (cognition and skill in promoting lifelong wellness) (Morrison, 1993)
> ➤ Approaches to sex and communicable disease (Morrison, 1993)

A Case Study—Fairness and Equality

One example of fairness and equality is the contested issue of competition. In writing his benchmark book, *No Contest: The Case against Competition*, Alfie Kohn (1986) wrote that competition is harmful to students. Kohn wrote that students learn that, to win, someone else has to lose. This message, Kohn suggests, is dysfunctional for a democracy because it is insular, non-representative of group process, and debilitating to creativity. Under what circumstances should a teacher promote competition? Should it be censured as poorly advocated for a school setting? What ways can content areas such as physical education use the topic of winning in a democratic manner? Perhaps the ability to win is really democratic. What issues related to **LF, JF,** and **EEO** are involved in making these decisions?

Consider elements of **LF, JF**, and **EEO** in reflecting on music, art, and physical education.

Strategies for Music, Art, and Physical Education

> ➤ Think about the type(s) of creativity your students portray.
> ➤ Vary assignments and plan thematically to include the affective, cognitive, and psychomotor domains in projects.
> ➤ Find community resources.
> ➤ Enlist the help of parents.
> ➤ Find corporate sponsors of projects.
> ➤ Think about a rubric for your arts curriculum.
> ➤ Expand your own experience with the arts.
> ➤ Determine the conditions for completion; discuss these with your administrator/grade or department and parents

Counselors: Academic, Career, and Special Needs

Students often find that they need special help with problems either in schoolwork or with relationships within school. Other students want support in trying to assimilate the information regarding university scholarships and entrance requirements. Public schools hire counselors with expertise and college degrees in areas such as business and psychology. These specialists have varied backgrounds. Some are school psychologists with degrees in this area, having spent years focusing on testing aptitude and ability. Others are more familiar with the process of aligning a student's abilities with those of a potential career. Important to all students is the scope and sequence both of the curriculum of the post-elementary years, and of electives taken in junior (or middle school) and senior high. The guidance a student receives from a counselor can preclude or encourage a life path and opportunity for advancement.

When parents are involved in the discussions of how a student will select courses, schools find that the student often makes appropriate choices and continues to find courses valuable. Some parents have had long-term experience with schools and know how to speak to administrators and counselors. They can easily act as an advocate for their student. Other parents are less familiar with the public school process and have little to no communication with schools. Thus, issues of **LF, JF,** and **EEO** can be found to alternatively support or reduce opportunity for students.

While many programs that test students have been normed or tried out on a large sample of students, often the tests themselves have been found to be representative of particular types of students. For example, language used in tests may be inconsistent with the language known and spoken by the student, and a skill such as math ability or higher-order thinking may be less highly scored on a test due to the barrier of language.

The issues of testing and counseling as a result of testing may be an area of **LF, JF,** and **EEO** that implies equality in student access. Do all students have equal access to the display of their skills? Are the media with which students demonstrate skill aligned with their abilities?

What role should the counselor take in helping students decide on a career? Should the parent be involved? What role should the school take in promoting the athletic abilities of some students over others? Should winning or high achievement be the bar that only potential college students must pass?

Reflect on issues of **LF, JF,** and **EEO** in thinking about counseling for career and academic development in coursework.

Strategies for Counseling and Referral to Counselors

➤ Review test scores.
➤ Learn about the different types of tests available.
➤ Have students re-tested periodically.
➤ Use classroom materials to support your case for a student's abilities.
➤ Add extra credit for effort in scoring students.

➢ View student abilities in multiple ways of knowing (Covey, 1989) and insist on testing in "multiple intelligences."

➢ Get to know the various counselors on your campus.

Observation of Special Education and Gifted Form

Focus on elements of LF, JF, and EEO.

What models of student placement are used (mainstreaming aides)?

Describe the lesson pace, presentation, and types of assignments.

Describe the lesson variance (extension of regular work, pursuit of personal interest).

What types of resources/support materials are used (community, site-based, other)?

What models of student support are used (peer tutors)?

Describe the classroom environment for student use.

Democratic Practice Reflection

Observation of Language Acquisition Form

Focus on elements of LF, JF, and EEO.

Describe the strategies of ESL and sheltered English that are used.

Describe how bilingual education is used in the content area.

Describe the use of schema building, modeling, and frequent clarification.

Describe the use of discourse (communication) and content focus.

Describe the type and level of interactive teaching.

Describe the environment for anxiety level and comprehensible input such as role-playing.

Describe how culture, values, and status are recognized.

Describe the level and type of parental and community involvement in discourse (conversation) about the value of the native language and culture and the learned language and culture.

Describe how bilingualism is encouraged.

Describe the strategies used to encourage biculturalism and cross-cultural respect.

Democratic Practice Reflection

Observation of Technology, Computers, and Software Form

Focus on elements of LF, JF, and EEO.

Describe the technological resources available in your district/school.

What resources and support (personnel, training) are available to the teacher?

Describe your use of the Internet to develop curriculum.

Describe how you involve student interests and needs in your Internet search for curriculum development.

What models of grouping are used in accessing technology (pairs, individual)?

Describe the involvement of volunteers, community, or parents in the use of technology.

Describe the type(s) of assignments used with technology (journal writing, e-mail).

Is the use of technology considered in evaluating projects or tests?

Is the software used aligned with the scope and sequence of curriculum development?

Democratic Practice Reflection

Observation of Technology, Computers, and Software Form

Focus on elements of LF, JF, and EEO.

Is the software used aligned with student understanding (context understandings)?

How are students engaged and involved in their own learning?

Is the use of technology scope/sequence and age-appropriate? Describe.

Is the program free of technical errors? How does it compare with other resources such as texts?

Describe student use (with teacher, with lab aide, with another student).

Democratic Practice Reflection

Observation of Counselors: Academic, Career, and Special Needs Form

Focus on elements of LF, JF, and EEO.

Describe your analysis of a student's test scores.

What types of tests are available in your district or school?

Are students re-tested periodically? If so, describe this.

What types of classroom materials (test, journals) can be used to support student abilities?

Is extra credit offered in scoring (evaluation of students)?

Describe the utilization of multiple ways of student knowing. Are tests offered in multiple intelligences?

Describe the counselors on your campus and their work with students.

Democratic Practice Reflection

Observation of Music, Art, and Physical Education Form

Focus on elements of LF, JF, and EEO.

List examples of student creativity.

How are assignments varied or planned thematically to include the affective, cognitive, and psychomotor domains?

Describe the use of community resources (parents, volunteers).

Describe the involvement of corporate sponsors of projects.

What type of rubric for evaluation is used in the arts curriculum?

How have you expanded your own experience and knowledge of the arts?

Under what circumstances is competition used? Who else in your district/school/community has discussed competition with the teacher?

Democratic Practice Reflection

Adjunct Activities

Recess and yard duty, school plays and events, parent conferences

What are the rules?

No pushing

No running

No talking

Liberty and Freedom   **Justice and Fairness**   **Equality and Equal Opportunity**

Visit an elementary school just as students are starting to arrive.

Where are the teachers? They may be at

Yard duty (the playground, the hallways or walks, the drop off points for cars and buses, the bicycle rack, the front office, school entry points, particularly unguarded or open spaces on playgrounds

Not so, high schools, you say?

Try the gym, the bleachers in sports areas, the student parking lot, the hallways, and the assistant principal's office.

Teachers could be in their rooms planning lessons, or in the teacher's lounge getting one more cup of coffee, or copying the last 100 pages of handouts. Sometimes they are doing these things, but often, several times a week most likely, they are involved in some type of campus routine that calls for teachers to insist on and then interpret a set of rules for student behavior outside of their own classrooms.

Schools make rules for safety first. Hoover and Kindsvatter (1997) write that most teachers view discipline negatively, considering it a "necessary evil of teaching that must be tolerated" (p. 1). The toleration appears somehow to be a visceral reaction to a truly negative experience. In presenting their text *Democratic Discipline,* Hoover and Kindsvatter hypothesize that, instead of viewing these responsibilities as negative and duties to be tolerated, view them as teaching (positive outcomes) that is grounded in "human relations as much as in authority" (p. 1). Thus, the philosophy of interaction for democratic practice is one of community rather than rule by might (the teacher's might, the school's might).

Rules can be generated to reflect a consensus of views. As in the case of a **democratic society**, it may be that the majority rules, and this majority independently creates the rules. Consensus assumes that all parties (parents, community, teachers, and students) have a voice in and contribute to the creation of school rules, particularly the consequences of breaking a school rule. In many cases, consensus does occur—all voices including the school board are heard. In practice, we may (as a majority) choose to refuse to follow rules, and as is often the case, the interpretation of rules is subjective to how the teacher views a student and then how he/she views the concept of safety.

It is also likely that the teacher's interpretation of who should follow rules (such as a teacher giving a student a warning "Don't run" or "YOU were running!") differs enough to ask us to pause and reflect on the issues of **LF, JF,** and **EEO.**

A Case Study

Eighth grader Jared loved the color black. Every day he picked out a T-shirt that had a black background. He wore his T-shirt long and baggy. He felt great, sort of grown-up. Watching him walk up to school in a dark black baggy shirt, Ms. Freestone thought Jared was portraying an attitude of defiance. School rules stated clearly no baggy shirts, no gang colors. Jared had been meeting four friends every morning in front of school. Ms. Freestone thought he was loitering in the halls. After standing around, exchanging greetings, the students walked off to class, and Jared, hoping to get out to football practice early, ran all the way out to the field.

Clearly a troublemaker, thought this teacher—no discipline, no respect for rules.

She phoned Jared's parents and told them he was causing trouble at school.

Jared's father asked what the school rules were. After hearing about the gang colors and baggy shirt, Jared's father asked, "Who made up these rules, anyway?"

Let's see if we can justify the need to create rules for students and then discipline democratically. First, it is important to understand that a "reasonable structure" (Hoover and Kindsvatter, 1997, p. 1) ensures a sense of safety for students. When students know the rules of a school, it is easier for them to know the limits of behavior and follow rules. However, the rules themselves require a review and understanding of the implications and assumptions of authority (rules). In what ways can we determine that the rules we create are representative of the values of a democracy?

Use this question to respond to the case study:

What Are the Goals of School Rules in a Democracy?

Civics education: Hoover and Kindsvatter (1997) wrote that our understanding of the way society is organizing our rule making and makes rules based on our understanding of this organization in part helps us construct rules for students in school.

> *...notions and technical aspects of how our democratic national government is organized and operates*
>
> (Hoover and Kindsvatter, 1997)

For example, we base our court system on the individual rights of man (to be treated fairly, to be brought to justice). School rules based on the understanding of how *our government operates in a civic manner* promote a system of democratic practice and allow teachers to share with students the justification, history, and policies of a democracy.

Character education (citizenship) refers to how people interact as members of a given community and how well they uphold the standards of the spirit and intent of certain laws and rules (Hoover and Kindsvatter, 1997, p. 73). The extent to which we adhere to these standards, as defined by a ruling body, determines how good a citizen we are (p. 73). Hoover and Kindsvatter have written that good citizens work for the benefit of collective standards, not only for their own well-being (p. 73). Thus, as we review rules such as *do not hit another student, even if justified*, we have to determine for ourselves and for students the conditions under which a citizen should uphold the rules. What if someone hit you first? What if they hit you and continue to do so? Should you hit back in order to get him/her to stop? Should you get four friends to beat this person up after school? Should you hit back and say nothing to a teacher?

Reflect on elements of **LF**, **JF**, and **EEO** in determining and enforcing school rules.

How will you help students define and act on the role of civics and character education in their own practice of democracy? If you are on a playground or in the hallway for a "duty" responsibility, how will you enforce the school rules?

Strategies for School Rules

➢ Create a student/teacher/parent committee to determine school rules.
➢ Give awards for following school rules.
➢ Base grades on citizenship.
➢ Use various forms of media to reinforce school rules (banner, newsletters).

Strategies for Civics and Character Education

➤ Develop a schoolwide curriculum that addresses both civics and character education.

➤ Create a club or an organization for honors in character.

➤ Base grades on citizenship.

➤ Create a student council or another organization that uses and learns about the rules of society (civics education).

➤ Organize a micro society or a schoolwide system of mock courts.

➤ Bring in various civics organizations to reinforce the values of a democratic society (e.g., working together to help society [Rotary Club, Lions club]) and have students create their own model that helps their school.

➤ Invite members of various professions such as doctors, nurses, police, and firefighters to demonstrate character and civic effort.

Special Events—Selecting Students for Team Sports and the School Play

Every school has events adjunct to the academic agenda—events such as school plays, talent shows, and spirit lines or cheer squads. When you observe these activities, think about how the students are selected to participate, and what rules are used to govern the events. For example, must students involved in competitive team sports ride on the school bus together? Should they all be required to attend practice but meet a certain grade point average to participate? Is it a rule that students have only day trips and no overnight trips? Why? Under what circumstances should teachers enforce rules for behavior?

Think about the selection process. Should only the best team players be selected for competitive sports? Should they all get to play? How about other events, such as school plays and shows? Which students should be allowed to participate? Who determines the rules?

Some school districts have found that the competition for some of these events is so great they have eliminated them. Events such as elections on school campuses can be very competitive. The student who becomes senior class president or school council president may be ranked higher than another student in the college application process. Is this fair? Do all students have equal access to campaign signs and resources? If not, who decides how these resources should be allocated?

Vote for Fred. He's Our Pres!

Mary Sue for Homecoming Queen!

Support Amy for Prom and Cheer!

> Think about **LF**, **JF**, and **EEO** in issues about special events.

Strategies for Selecting Students for Special Events

➤ Be certain to have a committee create a rubric (rules) for participation.

➤ Encourage all parents and businesses to support students.

➤ Find a role for every student to play.

➤ Vary the roles for all students to participate.

➤ Have students determine some of the roles such as equipment manager and scorekeeper.

➤ Pre-determine (with a committee) rules before an all-day/overnight trip.

➤ Ask administration and the district for guidelines for student participation and behavioral expectations (and consequences).

➤ When making an exception for a rule (particularity), be certain to explain the reason (Student B missed four practice sessions and CAN still play Friday night—reason: illness).

➤ Know the strengths and weaknesses of your students (skills, abilities, behavior, personalities).

Observation of School Rules: Character and Civic Behavior Form

Focus on elements of LF, JF, and EEO.

What type of governance committee exists for determining school rules?

Are school rules rewarded? How?

Are grades given for citizenship? How?

What type of media (buttons, banners, newsletters) is used to reinforce school rules?

How are the areas of civics and character education determined (committee, administrator, teacher alone)?

Are grades given for citizenship?

Do schoolwide organizations (e.g., student council) learn and practice rules of society (civics education)?

Is there a schoolwide event or construct (e.g., a micro society) that reinforces the values of a democratic society?

What civic organizations visit and speak at your school and support school rules?

Do members of community professions (e.g., nurses, police, firefighters) visit the school and model character and civic effort?

Democratic Practice Reflection

Observation of Special Events (Sports, Teams, and Plays) Form

Focus on elements of LF, JF, and EEO.

How was the rubric created for student participation in special events?

How does the community support students in special events?

To what extent do all students have the opportunity to participate?

Are students involved in determining the roles of students in special events?

How are rules determined for day or overnight trips?

What guidelines are there from either the district or the administrator regarding student participation in and behavioral expectations for special events?

When are exceptions made for a rule (specificity or exception to a rule)? Are reasons explained?

What does the teacher know about a student's demonstrated ability to participate?

Democratic Practice Reflection

District Policies, Government, and the Law

District Policies

School districts create policies for their schools. Members of a school district are elected (in some districts, members are appointed) to represent the public at large. This is similar to a general election that selects a representative to any other governing body such as the state legislature. These school district boards have the power to set policy for the schools within their area or districts. The board then elects its own president, who calls for board meetings and follows parliamentary procedure.

If parents, the community, teachers, or students want to speak to a board member regarding a school district policy, they may do so; however, the board convenes on a regular basis, and issues of policy are usually taken up in hearing before the full board. It is important to follow the prescribed procedure before addressing a board (such as bringing a petition to the board).

School boards may not violate governmental law. For example, they cannot discriminate in areas such as gender or race. They may not create a policy that violates civil law such as refusing to graduate a qualified student based on age.

They may, however, determine district policies and determine the consequences for an infraction against a policy. For example, if the school board has determined that a school has a no tolerance policy against weapons on school grounds and a student has brought a knife to school, the administrator or teacher may bring the student in contempt of district policy and act on this infraction. Students often claim that their rights have been impeded. In other words, if citizens of the state have the right to have a knife, why don't students have this right?

Courts have ruled that the primary business of schools is education, and disrupting (or potentially disrupting) the process of schooling is a violation of BOTH district and civil law. School boards may create policy that supports the continuance of the schooling process.

District policies vary in different parts of the country. Some districts require that all students buy their own books and the books are not refundable at the end of the school year. Other districts require school uniforms or disallow gang wear such as baggy pants or oversized shirts. Some districts will allow the administration of corporal punishment.

When reviewing the policies of your school district, think about the elements of **LF**, **JF**, and **EEO**.

Strategies of School District Policies

➢ Do the policies follow civil law?

➢ Has the board been elected or appointed according to the laws of the state governing board?

➢ Does the board have regular meetings and policies for the constituency to approach it?

➢ Does the board consider the needs and desires of its constituency in creating policy?

➢ Is the board knowledgeable about school law and government?

Government and the Law

The right to create, tax, support, and regulate schools is a function delegated to each state rather than a right of the Federal government. The responsibility for education rests with each individual state. Federal law impacts states' rights in the area of civil law such as discrimination. Most states have a state school board of education or a state superintendent of schools with a support staff.

The legislature determines which laws will govern the state's schools. For example, the legislature will determine if an exit test is needed to graduate from high school. In this case, after the state has determined that such a statute will be in effect, each school district must create policies for implementing the new state law. School districts will need to meet state law by accommodating students and supporting them in their effort to meet state graduation requirements.

The area of testing is often a source of debate. Many teachers do not feel the state can evaluate their students, school, or district well enough to determine the type of testing that benefits their community and community of students. The state usually is responding to the call for uniformity and measurement, for example a measurement to get into college, or uniformity in results from school that are supported by state funding.

Funding is a controversial area. Some districts have quite an array of materials, resources, and funding due to appraised property tax. Other districts have less highly appraised property and schools are less highly funded. State law requires that all schools are treated equally; thus, within a state, but in different districts, opportunity, fairness, and freedom are not equally treated. Some districts receive equal state funding but city or local school district funding is unequal. In these districts, supplies run out before the year is out, or funding for trips or extra events is low and is not well supported by the community. The issue of fairness in school funding has long been a topic for discussion.

Reflect on elements of **LF**, **JF**, and **EEO** and issues of government and the law.

Strategies for Reviewing Issues of Government and the Law

➢ Find out the goals and policies of your state department of education.

➢ Become familiar with your state laws regarding the regulation of schools', teachers', and parents' rights.

➢ Find out how state taxes support public education.

➢ Find out about regulations regarding bonds and local taxes.

➢ Review policies regarding testing of public school students.

➢ Find out about policies regarding alternative licensure of teachers.

➢ Find out the policies that regulate alternative forms of public education such as charter schools, vouchers, vocational or technical schools, alternative education, and home schooling.

➢ Find out about policies for achievement testing in your state.

Observation of District Policies Form

Focus on elements of LF, JF, and EEO.

Describe district policies and requirements of civil law.

Describe the manner of election/appointment and organization of the school district board of education.

What are the regulations regarding public participation in board meetings and procedures?

How is the public involved in creating school district policy?

What do you already know and what else would you like to know about school law and local and state government?

What are the district's policies regarding the continuance of employment (tenure laws)?

Democratic Practice Reflection

Observation of Government and the Law Form

Focus on elements of LF, JF, and EEO.

Describe the goals and policies of your state department of education.

What are the state laws regulating schools', teachers', and parents' rights?

How are state taxes used to fund public education?

What are the state laws regulating bonding and local taxes?

What policies are there at the state level regarding the various types of testing of public school students (special education, psychological testing)?

What policies does the state have for regulating alternative forms of public education such as charter schools, vouchers, vocational schools, and home schooling?

What is the state board of education's policy toward achievement testing?

Democratic Practice Reflection

Community and Business Participation

Parent Volunteers

Parents volunteer at school to help support the various activities, routines, or special events that add to the life of a school. For example, a school carnival, held after hours, but for the financial support of a school is often staffed by the many parent volunteers in the community. Parents also spend many hours on school sites, helping with various tasks and routines around school such as preparing copying material, creating various types of hands-on materials for projects (egg cartons, milk cartons, paper letters, numbers for projects), or overseeing a project such as categorizing books in the library. Parents with special skills such as computer skills can be found volunteering in the school's lab or tutoring students. Parents volunteer to tutor individual students or bring in extra help for fundraisers such as cookie sales.

Parents who volunteer in the classroom have an added responsibility of helping students and learning the teacher's routine. Sometimes they do not agree with the teacher or school program, and this can be seen as a parent who "shops" or reviews the work of a teacher in order to get a class that aligns with his/her perceived need for his/her own student. Teachers frown upon this type of parent involvement and consider this analysis as non-professional, yet isn't the school created for the parents as well as the children? Shouldn't parents be able to just stop by and volunteer their reflections and comments as well as their work?

Booster Clubs and Parent Clubs

These organizations are formed to bring financial support to the school. They run many types of fundraisers, from selling soda pop on the campus to selling hot dogs at a football game. Club members often raise very large sums of money and they are very loyal "boosters" of the campus, often after their own children have graduated from the system. However, they also have strong input into policy and the spending priorities of a school. For example, they may, with the band director and an assistant principal, decide to buy new band uniforms. Given the enormity of cost, most schools cannot do this by themselves. A booster club or parent club often becomes responsible for a two- to three-year project that can generate a large income. The clubs can be prestigious for parents, in the same way an alumni club can be prestigious for a university. Students of these participating parents can be thought of as a special group of well-liked students, in part due to the large amount of help their parents give and the "with-it-ness" or social understandings of parents. Imagine the feelings of a student whose parents have not been successful in their own schooling or are unfamiliar with schools and events at a school. How would this student feel?

Business Partnerships

Local businesses often support the community schools. Sometimes they donate their projects such as sandwiches and pop or t-shirts to a school. They donate money or door prizes such as a set of tires. Sometimes they provide resources such as computers or manpower such as engineers to work with students. Businesses have varied interests in supporting schools: (a) schools help create a new generation of potential buyers; (b) schools need help; and (c) Parents of the students may end up buying from these businesses because they have supported the schools. All in all, businesses support schools and do so to be a good neighbor and member of the community.

> Consider elements of **LF**, **JF**, and **EEO** in working with community volunteers.

Strategies for Working with Community Volunteers

> - Create a file folder of policy and procedure.
> - Prepare a welcoming breakfast for volunteers.
> - Show each volunteer what he/she is expected to do and how to do it.
> - Be certain the volunteer knows something about the scope and sequence of students at your grade level.
> - Be certain your volunteers understand regulations and laws regarding students and schools.
> - Be certain you do *not* leave a non-certified teacher with students without certified personnel such as a teacher or substitute.
> - Have materials ready, if possible, for volunteers.
> - Have the principal review and implement school policies.
> - Be prepared with suggestions for financial expenditures.
> - Be prepared to have the board of education vote on the use of funds.

Notes

Observation of Parent Volunteers, Booster and Parent Clubs, and Business Partnerships

Focus on elements of LF, JF, and EEO

Describe the work site available to volunteers.

What types of events do parents, the community, and volunteers create for students? Are they fair? What do they cost, and who supports this cost?

What is the school policy for parents visiting in the classroom?

What types of information are given to parents about all children as learners?

What types of aid to schools have businesses given to schools?

Parents are taxed for public schools. Should they be able to participate in all aspects of the school?

What role should business play in the life of a school? Describe its role.

Democratic Practice Reflection

Chapter 4

Preparing to Participate in Classrooms

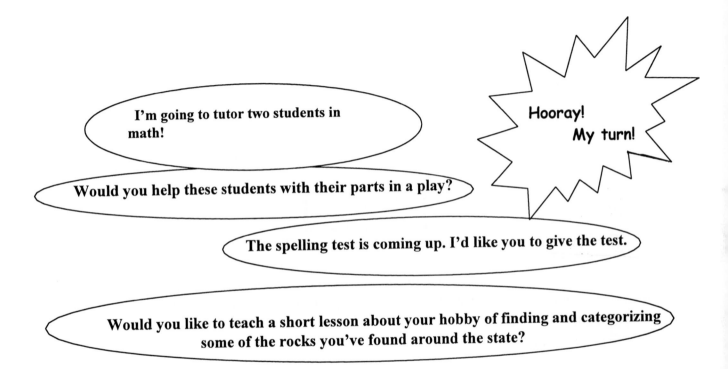

Planning to Participate!

In order to have a plan to participate in teaching either in small or large groups, it is important that you design a plan for implementation. This plan is termed a *lesson plan*. There are several ways to write lesson plans such as direct instruction, spiraled, or and integrated plan (see page 150). Every good lesson plan, however, contains some basic elements.

Elements of a Comprehensive Lesson Plan

➢ **The objective(s):** the goal(s) of the lesson; the measurable purpose or outcome of the lesson

➢ **An introduction,** also called a set or anticipatory set or motivation for the lesson

➢ **Instructional steps,** also called procedure or steps to the lesson

➢ **Closure,** also called summary

➢ **Application,** also called homework, assignments, or in-class guided practice

➢ **Evaluation,** also called testing or assessment

➢ **Resources,** or materials, or bibliographic information

➢ **Additional information:** notes to the teacher such as location of special materials such as lab equipment

➢ **Flexibility:** like all good plans, lesson plans need to be flexible and meet the diverse needs of all students

Writing a Lesson Plan

Objectives

The stated objective of a lesson describes the desired learner outcome for that lesson. For example, if the objective is for students to be able to describe various causes of the Civil War, then the teacher will write a lesson plan that promotes this outcome. In so doing, the teacher and students have a goal or an achievable/measurable purpose. The objective should be written with the following questions in mind.

Questions to Consider When Writing Measurable Objectives

➢ What do the students already know?

➢ What do they need to know?

➢ What are the multiple abilities of the students?

➢ Does the objective(s) consider the multiple domains of learning (affective, cognitive, and psychomotor)?

➢ How much can I teach in one planned period of time?

➢ Is the objective related to school, district, state, and national standards and goals?

➢ Is the objective related to the NCTS standards?

➢ Does the objective contain elements of democracy (**LF, JF, EEO**)?

Objectives may be written for various levels of cognition. One resource for writing objectives at increasingly higher levels of cognition is Bloom's Taxonomy. This guide to writing objectives (1956) uses verb forms to increase the level of understanding and demonstration of skill that can be expected for the learner. Examples of verb forms are

> ➢ The student will be able **to define** . . .
> ➢ The student will be able **to compare and contrast** . . .
> ➢ The student will be able **to analyze or synthesize** . . .

Examples of Objective(s) with Elements of Democracy

> ➢ The student will be able **to define** the terms *freedom* and *slavery* (**LF**).
> ➢ The student will be able **to compare/contrast** causes of the Civil War (**JF**).
> ➢ The student will be able **to analyze/synthesize** the viewpoints of the North and South during the Civil War (**EEO**).

Introduction/Anticipatory Set

The anticipatory set creates an overall tone for the lesson. It allows the teacher to create a netline with students' prior knowledge, to activate current knowledge or to motivate students about knowledge that will be part of the current lesson. These elements can be present in the introduction to a lesson. The introduction set can be very motivating for students. They can observe or participate in a new way of thinking or viewing something they will soon relate to when they are learning something new. Students who try out something new during the set can become very engaged in their own learning!

Elements to Consider When Writing the Introduction Set

> ➢ What do the students already know?
> ➢ What are the students interested in?
> ➢ What type of resources (such as maps, manipulatives, music) are available?
> ➢ What type of lesson will be taught (lab session, mapping skills, math practice)?
> ➢ Describe the length and amount of time for introduction set. What are the multiple abilities of the students?
> ➢ What learning domains should be considered (cognitive, psychomotor, kinesthetic)?
> ➢ What **elements of democracy** does the introduction set include (**LF, JF, EEO**)?

Examples of Introduction/Anticipatory Set with Elements of Democracy

➤ "Watch this light. It is coming from my flashlight! I also have a small radio turned on low. Listen to the music. What do you think? [LF] Do you know if light travels faster than sound?"

➤ "How many of you know how professional baseball teams are formed? Take one of these numbered cards and form your own teams of lab partners." (JF)

➤ "There are some new media centers in our room! Who would like to tell how they want to use the centers? Would you show me how you use media? Can I show you? What would you like to know?" (EEO)

Instructional Steps to the Lesson

The instructional steps to a lesson are a procedure designed by the teacher. Some procedures are found in teacher's guides to curriculum and adapted by teachers to their own class. The instructional steps direct how a teacher will teach and what the students will do during the lesson. In specifying the steps to a lesson, be certain to include the following elements:

Elements to Consider When Writing the Steps to a Lesson

> Are the steps of the lesson aligned with the objectives of the lesson?
> Will the students be able to accomplish the objectives if these instructional steps are followed?
> Are the steps listed in a logical sequence?
> Are transitions between steps logical and appropriate to achieving the objective?
> What are the students able to do?
> What are the multiple needs and abilities of the students?
> How much can I teach in one planned period of time?
> Do the **steps contain elements of democracy (LF, JF, EEO)**?

When writing the steps to the lesson, it is also important to remember to vary the types of lessons you teach. For example, you may want to have a discussion including various domains of learning (affective, cognitive, or psychomotor). The lesson plan procedures sometimes include various domains; thus, you may want to have a discussion, and then a hands-on lab or artwork activity. When planning for student procedures, this type of variation in a lesson can provide the opportunity for students to learn at multiple levels of understanding **(EEO)** as well as encourage students of all levels of understanding to participate **(JF)**.

Example of Instructional Steps to a Lesson with Elements of Democracy

> Bring in maps of Civil War battles.
> **Ask students to find** the battles that occurred by first finding the battle on a time line above the blackboard **(LF)**.
> Have students fill in their own time line **(LF)**.
> After the time line, **students lead (LF)** a discussion of which battles occurred first, which were last, and **why (JF)** each battle affected the outcome of the war.
> Ask students to describe in their journals **their vision of the effect (EEO)** of the battles on the outcome of the civil war.

Notes

Application and Practice

The application of concepts learned during the instructional steps to the lesson can lead to guided practice and student application. A variety of formats such as handouts with sample math problems or writing a poem are some types of guided practice. Thus, the practice is a way for a teacher to plan for student involvement in his/her own learning. Depending on how the teacher plans for this application (and practice), a student can also experience new learning or discovery of *how* a concept can be applied. Application and practice can be a creative process.

A Case Study

If a student uses a poem's format but then adds additional components such as rhythm or metaphor, the student is both applying a concept and still bringing his/her own interests to the application. This type of planning allows for all students to participate (**EEO**) and for individuals to be original (**LF**) and is encouraging to students at all levels of understanding and ability (**JF**).

Questions to Consider When Writing the Application/Practice Part of a Lesson Plan

> ➢ Is the application/practice related to the objective?
> ➢ Will the students be able to accomplish the application?
> ➢ What are the multiple needs and abilities of students?
> ➢ Can the application be accomplished in the planned amount of time?
> ➢ Does the application contain **elements of democracy (LF, JF, EEO)**?

It is important to encourage various types of application/practice. For example, a teacher may think of and ask students to contribute their ideas for application. The class can list several types of possible applications or practice. They can decide on dates or times the application will be due. Be certain to encourage and try out various types of applications.

Examples of Application and Practice of Instructional Steps in a Lesson Plan

➢ Use worksheets or ancillary materials (such as question sheets) from the textbook. **(JF)**
➢ Bring in artwork. **(LF)**
➢ Have students use art/create art. **(LF and JF, EEO)**
➢ Use graphs and charts (math). **(JF)**
➢ Use manipulatives such as wipe-off maps, overheads and projector, musical instruments, and non-art items such as beans for counters, sticky pads, lab dishes, indigenous plants and natural materials. **(LF)**
➢ Use technological support such as computers, video, tape recorders. **(LF)**
➢ Use both mastery (re-take tests) and discovery (learn by doing) models of application. **(JF, EEO)**

Closure in a Lesson Plan

To reinforce the instructional process as supportive of students as they learn, a section of the lesson plan is devoted to closure or synthesis of the lesson's *main points*. This is similar to a summary of the instructional steps that are needed to accomplish the objective. It may be that only one or two **key steps** are emphasized during the closure section. Either the teacher or students may create the closure. Sometimes a teacher will tell the students that they will summarize the lesson or instructional steps, and students follow this model. Otherwise, the closure is teacher-led.

Elements of Closure or Summary Techniques in a Lesson

➢ Is the closure related to the objective?
➢ Is the closure teacher-led?
➢ Are the students actively involved in leading their own closure?
➢ Can the student(s) show or tell how they will apply the instruction in the future?
➢ Is the information/process described brief and not drawn out in detail?
➢ Are visual aids involved in closure?
➢ Did the teacher transition between application to closure?
➢ What are the needs and abilities of the students?
➢ Is the lesson paced well so that closure is not forgotten in place of instruction? Do not let time run out and forget to complete the closure section.
➢ Does the closure section contain elements of democracy? **(LF, JF, and EEO)**

When writing the closure section of the lesson plan, be certain to vary the types of closure you are planning. You may want students to come up to the board and all write their answer to a problem. You may want them to question or make remarks to their study buddy, or the teacher may ask a few questions, using strategies of higher order thinking.

Example of Closure in a Lesson Plan

➢ Ask students to write two causes of the Civil War (on a sticky note) and pass their answer to their study buddy. **(EEO)**
➢ Have each student write their answers **(LF)** or write in pairs **(EEO)** at the board after a step to the lesson has been used.
➢ Use handouts/sheet work.
➢ Lead a discussion about the causes of the Civil War.
➢ Ask students to predict various outcomes of the Civil War based on the content of the day's lesson and have them write in their journals.

Resources for Lesson Plans

Resources of varying types adds to student's abilities to think about and try out new concepts and to think and probe old concepts in a new or interesting way. For example, math manipulatives give students a way to try out a concept they have read or heard about in the classroom. Providing students with materials that they can use is another way to support their individual freedom **(LF)**. They can become the discoverers of knowledge or can apply knowledge to a project. Thus, lesson plans that provide for the opportunity **(EEO)** to use materials additionally supports democratic practice.

Further, in creating opportunities to use various types of materials and resources, the teacher is fair **(JF)** to students of varying ability, as some students may be prepared for the use of resources in multiple levels of ability. One example of this variance is the use of technology. Some students may be knowledgeable about the use of word processing software, while other students may excel at using graphics software. Students may have little or no access to computers outside of their school or have not yet had exposure to some software programs. With insight into designing lesson plans with various types and levels of resources, a teacher can increase opportunity for all students to learn and advance at multiple levels of ability **(EEO)**.

Questions to Consider in Selecting Resources in a Lesson

➢ Are the resources aligned with the objective?
➢ Do the resources support and not overpower the objective?
➢ Are the resources available for students at multiple levels of ability?
➢ Are the students actively involved in the use of resources?
➢ Do the resources contain elements of **LF, JF,** and **EEO?**

Finding Resources

Resources can be commercially published products (such as multiplication flash cards, science kits, or reading handouts), or non-commercial materials (such as beans for counters, egg carton plant holders for science, or students' created literature books or stories). In any case, the resources a teacher uses in a lesson stimulate and enrich a classroom. Look for resources everywhere you go. Supermarkets and libraries are rich sources of materials that are sometimes donated to teachers and schools. Parents and community members often donate resources to teachers. Be certain to ask your school about its policy for donated items and the types of items it can accept. Some resources might require the use of electrical outlets or wiring that must be first updated. It is important to understand your district's policies of receiving gifts from businesses and soliciting for monetary donations. It may be that an issue of equality or equal opportunity underlies the policy of resources as a donation **(EEO)** in your district.

Examples of Resources in a Lesson Plan

➢ Ask students to bring in **(EEO)** older maps of the United States. Find the regions that mark Civil War battles.
➢ Ask a librarian for examples of music, clothing, or books about the Civil War.
➢ Find hands-on materials **(LF)** at places such as book or garage sales or used book stores.
➢ Ask a veteran's civic group to speak to your class about the group's collected materials from the Civil War era, including magazines with information.

Reflecting on Your Lesson Plan

After you have an opportunity to teach your lesson, reflect on and evaluate the plan:

Questions to Consider in Reflecting on Your Lesson Plan

➤ What was the strength of the lesson? What did you do or say to help students
➤ achieve the objective?
➤ What would you do differently? Why?
➤ What elements of the plan supported democratic practice (**LF, JF, EEO**)? Why?

Students' Own Involvement in Lesson Planning!

After you review your lesson plan form, evaluate your lesson with the students in your class! This type of evaluation or reflection allows for **LF**, since students have an opportunity to discuss their classroom procedures with their teacher. For example, if resource centers for manipulatives were part of your plan, how did you evaluate student achievement? What did the students think of the activity? Were they reaching their objective? How did they demonstrate what they know?

Students' Own Reflections on Democratic Practice!

Students who have been involved in a classroom lesson can help a teacher reflect on democratic practice by giving the teacher and their classmates feedback about what they learned and why. For example, a student might suggest they develop some maps of their own instead of looking at prepared maps and in so doing give feedback regarding **LF** to their teacher. The teacher could adjust the lesson plans to meet the needs of students (**JF**), and all students could benefit from the opportunity to reflect on what works well for their classroom (**EEO**). Why is it important to ask students what they did that was successful in their own learning and what they would do (or have a teacher do) differently?

By involving students in their own reflection on democratic practice, they live and learn about the process in action. The reflection becomes the democracy!

Advice from Your Mentor-Teacher

Your mentor-teacher has observed classrooms for a long time. He/she has tried multiple methods of working with students. *Ask your mentor-teacher to reflect with you* about your lesson plan.

Questions for Reflection with a Mentor-Teacher

➢ What did I say or do to support student learning?
➢ What did I say or do that could be taught differently?
➢ What feedback from students and democratic practice is valid for this lesson?
➢ What elements of democratic practice (**LF, JF, EEO**) were found in my lesson?
➢ **How could I revise my plan to strengthen democratic practice?**

Notes

Form for Writing Lesson Plans

Focus on elements of LF, JF, and EEO.

Objectives of the lesson
>   Describe the objectives' link to school, district, state, and national goals.
>   Describe the objectives' link to the NBPTS—Social Studies-History standards.

Introduction/Anticipatory Set
>   Describe how you will include and motivate student interests, abilities, and skills.

Instructional Steps
>   Describe the steps to the lesson. Are these steps aligned with the lesson objectives?
>   Note the steps that include meeting the multiple needs/abilities of students.

Application/Practice
>   Is the application or practice related to the objectives?
>   Note the steps or process of the application/practice that meets the multiple needs and abilities of students.

Closure
>   Is the closure related to the objectives? Does it summarize the lesson information?
>   Are the students involved in the closure?

Resources
>   Are the resources aligned with the objectives?
>   Are resources provided for learners at all levels of ability?

Reflection on the Lesson
>   What was the strength of the lesson? What were the weaknesses of the lesson?
>   Describe the students' and mentor -teacher's reflection on the lesson.

Part Three

What Is Democratic Practice in Schools?

- **Chapter One**
  Making Sense of Democratic Practice

- **Chapter Two**
  Building the Future of Democracy

- **Chapter Three**
  Applications of the Roots of Democracy

- **Chapter Four**
  Writing a Philosophy Statement of Democratic Educational Beliefs

- **Chapter Five**
  Summary

![Chapter heading bar]

Making Sense of Democratic Practice

Locating and Analyzing Democratic Concepts in Your Observation Form

Step One: Finding the Theme

> ➤ Review your observation form.
> ➤ **Find the main theme** in each observation. Is it liberty and freedom **(LF)**? justice and fairness **(JF)**? equality and equal opportunity **(EEO)**?
> ➤ Use a highlight pen to identify this theme.

Step Two: Using Initials

> ➤ **Use the initials** that represent each theme and write those initials by the theme in the observation guide.
> ➤ You may find **more than one theme**. For example, you may find **LF** more than once, or you may find several themes such as **LF** and **JF**. If you find more than one theme, indicate each theme using the initials next to the highlighted section.

Sample Observation Form Entry

The teacher asked students which storybook **they wanted to hear (LF)** her read. **She listened (EEO)** to suggestions from many children. Then, **the children voted (JF)** on the book they wanted to hear. After the story was read, students described what they liked best in the story. The teacher tried to involve her students in the selection of materials as much as possible. **Liberty and Freedom (LF)**

Step Three: Finding the Key Words

> ➤ **Find the key words** in the areas highlighted in your observation form.
> ➤ **Describe the themes**, telling **why each theme** in the example demonstrates liberty and freedom for the students.

Sample Observation Form Entry with Key Words
- ♦ They **wanted** to hear: The student's interests are met.
- ♦ She **listened**: The student's interests are voiced and heard.
- ♦ **Children voted**: Democratic representation of student choice.

Step Four: Identifying the Key Element(s)
- ➤ **Identify an element of democratic practice** in the observation entry and tell why this element represents democratic practice.
- ➤ Continue to **identify and describe** each key element with each key word.

Sample Observation Form Entry with Elements of Democracy (LF, JF, or EEO)
They wanted - students express their interests and the teacher responds to these interests. The focus of teacher-developed curriculum is based on the interests of the students. **(LF)**
She listened - When the teacher listens to students, they are given an equal opportunity to participate in class discussion. **(EEO)**
Children voted - When students have a voice in their classroom, they are empowered and feel that the class practice is just. **(JF)**

Reflecting on Democratic Practice

Steps to Reflecting on Observations Forms Using the Democratic Discourse Model

---

- ➤ Review your observation form.
- ➤ What area of the model did the teacher emphasize? What area of the model would you change? Why? **Identify elements of LF, JF, and/or EEO.** Use the initials T for teacher activity, C for change you would make.
- ➤ What type(s) of discourse did you observe between teacher and student? student to student? student to resource (such as technology)? Where does this discourse fit into the model? **Identify elements of LF, JF, and/or EEO.** Identify T for teacher or C for change.
- ➤ How was the curriculum evaluated? Where in the model is curriculum evaluated?
- ➤ Identify elements of **LF, JF, or EEO.** Identify T for teacher or C for change.
- ➤ Describe the opportunity for interaction between student and teacher. Where is this located in the model? Identify elements of **LF, JF, and/or EEO.** Identify T for teacher or C for Change.

> Describe achievement/attainment in the observation. Where is attainment found in the model? Identify elements of **LF, JF,** and **EEO.** Identify T for Teacher and C for change.

National Standards for Teaching Social Studies—History

The NBPTS Board for excellence in teaching social studies and history has developed standards than can be aligned with elements of **LF, JF,** and **EEO** on your observation form. You can find the source of some of these standards in the democratic discourse model.

> Identify the observed element of teaching *(the teacher listened).*
> Identify the source of the element on the **democratic discourse model** *(Teacher draws on Taba model of curriculum development).*
> Link the element of observed teaching, the source on the **democratic discourse model,** and the **NBPTS teaching standard** in Appendix A.
> Write the teaching element, the DDM element, and the teaching standard at the **bottom of the analysis form (see pgs 146-47).**
> List the elements of democratic practice: **LF, JF,** and **EEO.**

Identifying Themes of Democracy

> Notice the themes that are used most often.
> Are they **LF, JF,** or **EEO**?
> What elements of democratic practice are most used, least used?
> Write the most and least used elements on the bottom of your analysis form.
> Determine a theme for the lesson. Determine a secondary theme.

Sample Observation Form: Identifying Themes and Organizing Data

Reflections on Observation and DDM
(Sample) The teacher emphasized the area of use of cooperative learning centers in the lesson. In the DDM, this area is student interaction and participation through discourse. *JF*

Continue with steps
National Standards for Teaching Social Studies—History
The observed element of the use of centers demonstrates (discourse) as *JF* and is found in Standard 5-
Promoting social understanding-Promotion of the social aspects of the human condition, physical environment, cultural settings and emerging trends for the future.
Continue with Steps

> **Collapsing the Themes of an Observation**
> The main theme of **democracy** in this observed lesson was **Justice and Fairness (JF)**. Secondary theme(s) of **LF** or **EEO** were or were not found.

Application of the Model of Democratic Discourse Form

Identify elements of LF, JF, and EEO.

Use the letters T for teacher activity and C for changes you would make.

What area did the teacher emphasize? What area(s) of the model would you change? Why?

What type(s) of discourse did you observe? Identify elements of the discourse.

How was the curriculum evaluated? Where in the democratic discourse model is curriculum evaluated?

Describe the opportunity for interaction between student and teacher. Where is this located in the model?

Describe students' achievement/attainment in your observation. Where is this type of attainment found in the model?

Application of the National Standards for Teaching Social Studies—History Form

---

Identify elements of LF, JF, and EEO

List the observed elements of teaching *(the teacher listened)*.

Identify the *source* of the teaching element on the democratic discourse model *(teacher uses the Taba model of curriculum development)*.

Link the element of observed teaching, the source on the Democratic Discourse Model, and find the National Board teaching standard.

Write the observed teaching element, the democratic discourse model element, and the National Board teaching standard. List the elements of **LF, JF, EEO** and show where they are found in this statement.

Organizing Data/Identifying Themes of Democracy Form

My Reflections on Observation and Democratic Discourse Model
In this section, re-write an identified area of democracy (**LF, JF,** or **EEO**) from
your observation. Reflect on how this area is important to democracy and how it aligns
with the Democratic Discourse Model.

National Standards for Teaching Social Studies—History
Reflect on the importance of the observed element of democracy and how it may align
to the standards taught. For example, does the element promote social understanding?
Why is this important in the element of democracy that you have observed?

Collapse the Theme(s) of the Observation
Notice the frequency of the identified themes. For example, does **JF** appear as the
identified element several times? Does it appear in the observed lesson several times?
Are there secondary themes of democracy (e.g., **LF** or **EEO**)? Summarize the evidenced
theme and the sub-topic found.

Chapter 2

Building the Future of Democracy

Reflecting on the Roles and Goals of Schools and Society

Constructs for the Future: Implications for Technology and Society

No discussion of future application or interest in a democratic nation can easily proceed without reflecting on the implications of the tools of the future—technology. Clearly, the ability to access and question information is more available to learners (and teachers) who have access (and training) to today's technological tools. Social stratification, or ordering of status in a society, may now be more dependent than ever upon the combination of access to and utilization of information. Teaching students the application of reason (vis-à-vis higher order thinking skills) that allows students to make sense of information, however, is quite another task. Thus, as teachers plan and teach lessons, they seek out new resources to help them create their lessons and they are informed by as well as **formed by** their use of technology.

One way to see how technology influences the form of a democracy is to examine the issue of justice and fairness in the distribution of computers and high-tech school buildings. Clearly, there is an uneven distribution of resources in school districts. There may be an aligned unevenness in the training of teachers who use computers and software. Teachers themselves may vary in their philosophies or approaches to teaching (Soltis, 1998; Stamm & Wactler, 1997). As teachers try out various forms of technology, they may also find their approaches to teaching shifting and changing. Doll (1993) writes that, in the ever-changing post-modern world, uncertainty causes stress, both to an individual and to the society in which this chaos appears as normative. In order to make sense of an approach to teaching (Wactler, 1990), to understand an individual's philosophy of education, it is important that students of education (and their mentors) become familiar with ways in which teachers can choose to approach their teaching and organize their classrooms.

A teacher may find that elements of democracy exist in each philosophical approach to teaching and the use of technology. Technology can be viewed alternatively as a helpful tool and not only as an agent of change. As teachers review assumptions in teaching philosophy, they may change their own approach to classroom practice. To this end, it is important that we review philosophies of education.

The next part of this section will present the following topics for the reader to consider as he/she begins to build an individual philosophy of democratic education:

➢ Responsibilities of Citizenship
➢ Value of Historical Concepts
➢ Review of the National Board for Professional Teaching Standards: History and Social Studies Standards

Building an Individual Philosophy of Democratic Education

A Historical Perspective

In order to construct a format for deciding upon the responsibilities of teachers to education, and of education to its citizens, it is important to take one more look at our definition of democracy.

It is expected that from our definition(s) we will then turn to creating a list of those values of character and responsibility reflective of a community that supports a democracy. In so doing, we list the responsibilities we have to these values and, thus, the responsibilities of citizenship.

Thomas Jefferson — A citizen's responsibility is to become educated. It does not rest easy with teachers, to command students to respond to a list of personal behaviors. Perhaps the best way to determine how students can learn about behavior and the responsibility one has to democratic principles is to review these principles historically and then determine how they can become a part of a student's experience at school. For Jefferson, the historical premise upon which a democratic nation bases its need for public schools is the crusade again ignorance (Wactler, 1997). Credited for arguing for this crusade, Jefferson wrote:

Preach, my dear Sir, a crusade against ignorance; establish and improve the law for educating the common people. Let our countrymen know that the people alone can protect us against these evils, and that the tax which will be paid for this purpose is not more than the thousandth part of what will be paid to kings, priests, and nobles who will rise up among us if we leave the people in ignorance.
(Ravitch, 1984, p. xi)

The focus of Jefferson's description of the importance of a well-educated citizen aligns with current writing regarding the need for high attainment (Bennett, 1991). Examples of practices aligned with attainment in democratic schools are assessment and standardized testing, grading, and high school exit and/or college entrance exams.

What impact does Jefferson's ideas about a democracy have on the goals of education and democratic practice in schools?

Benjamin Franklin — A citizen's contribution is to the needs of society. In an earlier paper defining the attributes of a democracy, Wactler (1998) wrote that democracy appears to be a social creation—that is, a type of governmental organization that recognizes **both** the independence of human beings and the needs of society. This centricity or intending toward the interests of a large social group is expressed in the following work of Benjamin Franklin:

> *When you assemble a number of men to have the advantage of their joint wisdom you inevitably assemble with those men all their prejudices, their passions, their errors of opinion, their local interests, and their selfish views. From such an assembly can a perfect production be expected?*
>
> (Ravitch, 1992, p.111)

Apparently, Franklin recognized the multiple perspectives of both the individual and the wants and needs of society. One example of this type of duality, as found in schools, is the notion of developing a curriculum for learners of all levels of ability. Some students may learn to read faster, or with greater depth. For a teacher considering these multiple abilities, both an individual's ability and those of the group as a whole are a consideration in designing units. For grading the class work, these same concerns may surface, some students achieving at higher levels versus the need of a school to reach curriculum goals.

What impact does Franklin's view of democracy have on the goals of education and on democratic practice in schools?

Jean-Jacques Rousseau — A citizen's personal freedom is an a priori gift of nature. Key to a discussion of democracy is the argument for personal freedom. Rousseau proposed that freedom is essential to a democracy, as it is the essential element of a democracy (Ravitch, 1992). In other words, if the citizens of a democracy do not feel free, and have the construct to act freely, then the order of government is not democratic. To give away one's personal freedom to the dictates of government is aligned with giving away those possessions of human institution (e.g., it is simply not possible to give away personal freedom, and it is degrading to a democracy to so insist). Rousseau wrote:

> *It would offend nature and reason to renounce them whatever the price. But if one could alienate his freedom like his goods, there would be a very great difference for those who enjoy the father's goods only by transmissions of his right; whereas since freedom is a gift they receive from nature [emphasis added] by being men, their parents did not have any right to divest them of it.*
>
> (Ravitch, 1992, p. 50)

One argument for personal freedom within a democracy is found in Rousseau's *Discourse on the Origin and Foundations of Inequality* (from *On the Social Contract* [Ravitch, 1992]). Writing in support of individual freedom, Rousseau contended, is not the opposite of arguing against the dispersion of power; rather, the need is for individuals to opportune themselves with their natural right to freedom (Ravitch, 1992, p. 50). In reviewing the needs of students in schools, it may also be stated (Wactler, 1998) that it is a right dear to many of the founders of American democracy.

What impact do Rousseau's ideas about democracy have on the goals of education and democratic practice in schools?

Responsibilities of Citizenship

Personal freedom and individual rights, however, are not independent of recognition of social relevance. Writing that political participation can be understood only through this social relevance is the inclusionary stance of John Locke. Locke in 1690 wrote that in a **civil society** one gives up freedom for the good of society or the commonwealth (Ravitch, 1992). As the individual consciously gives up freedom, he/she enters into a contract that benefits all of society as one people. However, this contract of giving of freedom is consensual; that is, it is by the consent of the governed that one gives up freedom. Wactler (1998) explained this relationship:

> *It is the execution of free will that one gives to the body politic, their enjoined representative power. In other words, one authorizes the government to govern for the good of one people. Individuals trust that their voice will be heard, that their natural right to freedom will not be undermined, and that the body at all times, recognizes that it governs only with this constancy, and not through an assumed dominion*
>
> (p. 5)

Given, then, that individuals give up some freedom for the good of society, what other responsibilities do they also have to their society, a democratic society?

A 1998 report from the Council on Civil Society (Institute of American Values) finds that a democracy needs not only common moral truths but also participation of its citizens in acting on these truths. The report appeals to the "American experiment in self government" and lists areas of civic participation that support a philosophy and commitment to "freedom and justice for all" (p.3).

In this report, a proposition for a civil society, a society of participatory citizenship rests on the following conceptual framework described as "our foundational sources of competence, character, and citizenship" (p. 3).

Council on Civil Society—Propositions for Democratic Citizenship

> ➤ The family (as a source of initial learning)
> ➤ Local community or neighborhood (safety and a common life)
> ➤ Civic organization (dispersed authority and pluralism)
> ➤ Art and art institutions (good craftsmanship, creativity, and expression)
> ➤ Local government (participatory local government, civic responsibility, skills of citizenship [deliberation, compromise, consensus building, and reason giving]).

Primary and Secondary Education

Nourish a common culture, intellectual skills, personal responsibility, respect for authority, respect for students and each other, civic literacy and knowledge of a constitutional heritage, respect for the lives of national heroes, definition of good citizenship, appreciation of society's civic and moral ideals (p. 10).

Higher Education

Intellectual freedom, reason and the scientific method, objectivity of truth and knowledge, diffusion of knowledge contribute to civic virtue (p. 10).

> ➤ Business, labor, and economic institutions: self-interest as well as service, cooperation with others and the common good.
> ➤ Media institutions: requires parental monitor to encourage civic responsibility and engagement
> ➤ Shared civic faith and a common civic purpose.
> > ◆ Citizens combine the private pursuit of happiness with devotion to the public good (p. 12).
> > ◆ Liberty, guided by the proposition that all people are created equal
> > ◆ Republican self-governance
> > ◆ Juridical principles of the American Constitution (p. 12)
> ➤ Public moral philosophy
> > ◆ Transcend selfishness
> > ◆ Freedom as a primary civic end
> > ◆ Political freedom—relativize the political domain and limit the power of the state
> > ◆ Human dignity as self-evident (p. 13)

What is the impact of these propositions for citizens in a democracy? **Think about the elements of LF, JF, and EEO.**

National Board for Professional Teaching Standards—Teaching Social Studies—History

Think about your ideas about democratic classroom practice (how you want to arrange your classroom, give grades, find out about student interests and attainment). Here are some guidelines for answering the questions of local and national interests.

> ➢ How will you meet the needs of national standards and local community?
> ➢ What are the approaches to teaching that you can select from?
> ➢ What is the historical basis for your determination?
> ➢ How can you align the National Board for Professional Teaching Standards (Social Studies-History) with local and state policy for students in schools?

Review of the NBPT Standards—See Also Part One and Appendix A

> ➢ Preparing for Student Learning
> ➢ Advancing Student Learning
> ➢ Supporting Student Learning

What are the elements of **LF**, **JF**, and **EEO** evidenced in these standards?

Chapter 3

Applications of the Roots of Democracy

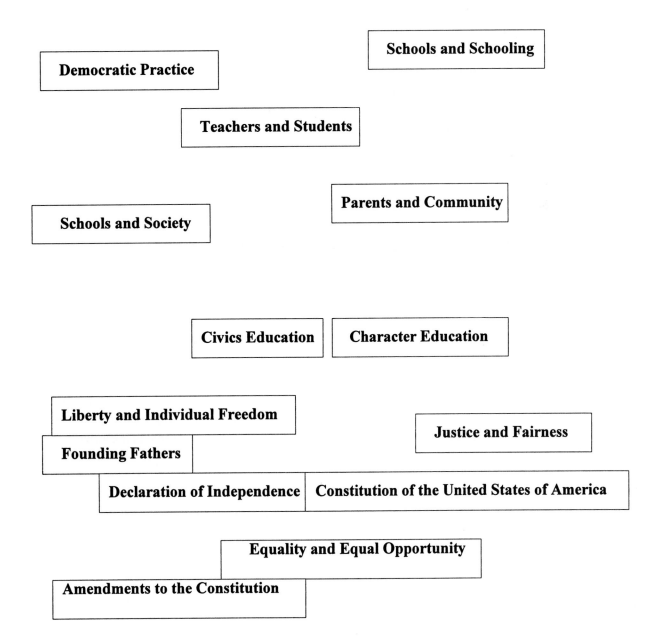

A Case Study

Liberty and Individual Freedom

Concept for Application: Under what circumstances should students be able to question the practices and rules in their classroom?

River Elementary School

The students in Mrs. Adams's fifth grade class at River Elementary School are beginning to question some of their class rules. The students are studying the origins of the American Constitution and the concept of a representative government. The legislative branch of government, they learn, has the explicit power to create new laws. Students have been asked to write a list of rules they think are fair and to then justify their answers. The objective of this lesson is for students to be able to describe the Lockian concept for the governed to have input (give consent) into their own rule and to explore how this concept is evidenced in American democracy and then in their own classroom.

Four students object to the rule that states no drinks of water during class. The rule was intended to keep the majority of students seated during class time. The teacher created the rule, and the reasons for the rule, then **told** students. The students had heard this rule in other classes, so they were familiar with it. They also were old enough to remember to get drinks of water before class starts. The four students who objected were not having difficulty in class or disturbing the class during discussion. They just didn't think rules should be made without their consent and their vote.

Mrs. Adams thinks she has done a good job in explaining both the rule and the reason for the rule. She's never had a problem with this rule before. However, now she has also taught the curriculum unit on self-rule and individual freedom (Liberty). The students believed in her descriptions that a monarchy is a state where citizens of the state (students) must follow the authority and rule of a monarch. They believe that a democracy allows citizens the liberty to create their own rules.

They want bottles of water at each desk so they can drink from them during class. They want no consequences for getting up to refill a bottle or get a drink. In other words, they want to be free.

Reflection on Practice

Sample Extended Questions

- How does **liberty and freedom** apply in this case?
- What decisions did the teacher make that helped students (the majority) stay on task?
- What decisions did the teacher make that represented what was historically a democratic action?
- Were the students correct in asking the teacher for representation in the rules and consequences in their room?

Students' Role in Questioning

- Is the consent of the governed a necessary argument for individual freedom?
- Is it appropriate for students to have this type of freedom in school?

Think about issues of **Liberty and Individual Freedom.**

Answer the sample extended questions above and describe the students' role in questioning rules in the classroom.

Compare your answer with that of another student. What do you think of his/her answer?

Strengths of his/her answer:

Strengths of your answer:

Example Curriculum Project

> Think about issues of **Liberty** and **Individual Freedom**.

Individual in History: Plato

Theme: Social stratification versus individualism democracy. When individuals **descend** from self-interest to communal need, their perceptions of democracy may predict the demise of liberty in a democracy. Students can practice this balance in the following project.

Students review issues surrounding the causes of the Civil War. They divide into focus groups, and each group selects a topic such as economics, social concerns, or rights of women. They have time in class to divide into these groups and to debate/review the positions of their classmates. Later they report their debate and conclusions in a large group discussion. This type of practice allows for individual input in small sessions that focus on each student's knowledge and interests.

Students can begin to analyze the view of others before they present in class.

The activities below are designed to promote LF in the classroom:

➢ Use a sticky note and have **students write one cause** of the Civil War. Each student then places the sticky note on a chart headed by a topic such as economics or social concerns.

➢ Have students create their own **debate board**. Using sticky notes, students write the positive and negative effects of each element in their topic area.

➢ Have **students conduct research on the Internet** and **debate and discuss** their findings.

➢ Encourage the use of **various print data** such as the daily newspaper and magazines.

➢ Create a news board for articles to be posted.

➢ Have students create their own "town halls" with debate and open meetings.

➢ Have **students write a role-play debate** between opposing viewpoints.

➢ Assume the **role of facilitator** and intervene in the debate only for the purpose of mediating rules of debate.

➢ Have **students decide** on the type of projects to represent their group for evaluation and grading. Projects include journal writing, portfolio making, essay writing, scoring on debates, and visual aids such as maps and overheads.

➢ **Create a rubric for grading, along with students.**

➢ **Invite parents to class to speak, debate, or observe.**

> ➢ **Community and business members are invited to class to speak, debate, or observe.**

What other activities can you add to this curriculum unit that will promote liberty or freedom?

$$\boxed{\textbf{Example of Classroom Practice}}$$

The activities below can be tried in your mentor-teacher's classroom. After you have tried one of these practices, reflect on elements of LF, JF, and EEO.

➢ Students bring their own materials such as sticky notes, overheads, notepaper and markers.
➢ Students rearrange the classroom environment and create a table or center for working in groups.
➢ Teacher sits with students in their groups and approaches the role of teacher as facilitator.
➢ Students design a computer center in their room and create a rubric for use of the Internet.
➢ Students invite special guests into class and provide a forum for discussion/debate.
➢ Students write to newspaper and magazine editors with their opinions.
➢ Students create their own debate team. They create the rules of debate.
➢ Students create their own court of justice and rules for the court to administer.
➢ Teacher creates a rubric for rules for the debate team and the court system.
➢ Students have a guest sit with them during class.
➢ Students peer edit and coach their team members.
➢ Students determine how to represent their best work for evaluation.
➢ Teacher decides on a rubric (with students) for examples that qualify for best work.
➢ Students create a "family circle" or "community circle" for class discussion.
➢ Parents decide to have a class discussion regarding class rules.
➢ Administrators decide to debate with students.
➢ Rules become part of debate.

What other types of classroom practices can you think of that demonstrate **liberty and freedom** for this curriculum unit?

155

Applied Project

Reflect on themes of **liberty and freedom** in democratic practice and create a scenario or case study of your own. Think about the elements of liberty in the case about drinking water in class. What other rules have you observed?

Compare your response with that of another student. Peer review and reflect.

Strength of his/her answer:

Strength of your answer:

A Case Study

Justice and Fairness

Concept for Application: Under what circumstances are student career opportunities promoted in a fair and just manner? What are the needs of the individual and what are the needs of society?

Mountain High School

Students in this high school are beginning to explore career opportunities. The school has a variety of methods of organizing the curriculum, often thought of as a tracking system. Students with college-bound goals have courses with a high degree of difficulty, while those students with goals for a business career or even non-defined goals have the same classes with a lower level of expected attainment.

The high school is having "career" week. Students are asked to create a career folder. They explore a variety of careers on the Internet and invite guest speakers to come to class. Some of these speakers discuss how they were encouraged to start their careers. Students initiate a career day fair at the school and invite the community to attend. Several technology businesses responded to student requests to attend the fair. The students reflect on their perceptions of their own career potential by writing in journals.

In Mr. Smith's English for Seniors course, several students volunteer to read aloud from their journals. One student wrote that he had been inspired by the speaker from the county attorney's office and would like to become an attorney. He believes that public service and helping the people of a community are great goals! Another student in Mr. Smith's class has determined that she wants to go to a vocational school, or even a community college, to be trained with computers and software design. The teacher remains silent during these journal readings.

After the day's class, the principal receives two phone calls. The parents of the students who read their journals aloud discovered that their students had not had the high school preparation for college, nor the guidance they should have had to help them understand how to select courses appropriate to computer careers. The principal does not expect teachers to give this guidance, but the career day has certainly opened up the issue of curriculum design and the justice/fair focus. For example, no one has told parents that electing courses means tracking student's options. The school guidance department feels that students tend to select classes they want, and society needs all types of employees.

This last argument is the functionalist/executive (Soltis, 1992; see Part Three in this text, p. 165) approach, which allows society to reap the reward of each individual's selection in a free-

157

market society. However, the school board now wants the high school to review student counseling methods to be certain that school course selection is just and fair, even if that means changing the school curriculum to require that all students take the same basic courses. It would take a great deal of extra money to hire more teachers and expand opportunity to offer higher status classes to all students.

Reflection on Practice

Sample Extended Questions

- What do you think is a fair and just solution to coursework and curriculum design?
- Is it fair to have some students in college-bound courses and others in vocational courses?
- Since it is expensive to hire more teachers, what other solutions are there, if any?
- Should the needs of society supplant the needs of the individual? What is fair? What is just?

Notes

Students' Role in Questioning

> ➤ Should the tendency for independence be supplanted by the needs of society?
> ➤ How should independence be balanced by social need?

> Think about issues of **Justice and Fairness.**

Answer the questions above and describe the role of the teacher in determining school policy for course work and curriculum design.

Compare your answer with that of another student. What do you think of his/her answer?

Strengths of his/her answer:

Strengths of your answer:

Example Curriculum Project

Think about issues of **Justice and Fairness.**

Individual in History: Protagoras
Theme: If properly taught, humans can demonstrate virtue and intelligence in the governing process. He can learn what is right and lawful. They can learn what is good and we all benefit from fair dealing.

Students have created their own career portfolio. The students have attended a career day fair at their school and invited members of their community to speak. Several technology companies and businesses responded to their requests. Some of these speakers spoke about how they were encouraged to start their careers. The students began to reflect on their perceptions of careers and are writing in their journals. They will explore a variety of careers on the Internet and start to write to the businesses in the community. *Students begin to analyze the direction of their own career and make personal choices.*

The activities below are designed to promote JF in the classroom. Try some of these activities in your mentor-teacher classroom.
 ➢ Have students bring in files and file folders to coordinate their data collection from newspapers and magazines.
 ➢ Have students invite family members or neighbors to class to speak about their careers.
 ➢ Have students invite other teachers in to find out about the profession of teaching.
 ➢ Encourage the use of the Internet for job and information searches.
 ➢ Encourage the use of student peer coaching to exchange materials found.
 ➢ Have students role-play their selected job or profession.
 ➢ Have students create their own "job board" representing various careers.
 ➢ Have students write the title of their favored job or profession on a sticky note and place these on a "job board." Students of like selections should help fill in information for that "job board."
 ➢ Assume the role of the facilitator and intervene only in group discussions when opinions or information is sought. Be a resource/guide.
 ➢ Teacher and students create a rubric for grading.
 ➢ Have students decide on the type of projects to represent their own work for grading. Projects include journal writing, portfolio making, essay writing, scoring on job role-play, and visual aids such as magazine or newspaper ads reviewed and analyzed.

What other activities can you add to this curriculum unit that will promote fairness and justice?

Examples of Classroom Practice

The activities below can be tried in your mentor-teacher classroom.

➢ Students bring in their own materials such as video cameras to tape role-play activity.
➢ Students re-design the classroom, finding storage space for materials collected.
➢ Teacher moves to each student or group to facilitate learning.
➢ Students decide if they want a computer center or individual sites for computers, and they create their own rubric for use of the Internet (following district guidelines).
➢ Students invite guests to class and provide a community/group setting for discussion.
➢ Students create their own newspaper and write want ads for jobs. They also write to local newspapers for advice about how to write an ad.
➢ Students create their own mock job interview team and role-play interviews. They determine which candidate is selected for a job and the rubric for selection.
➢ Teacher acts as facilitator for student-created rubric for rules of the mock interviews.
➢ Students shadow a job performed on or off the school site and report the attributes of the job.
➢ Students peer review the findings of other students.
➢ Students determine how to best represent their work for evaluation.
➢ Teacher co-creates the rubric for examples that qualify for best work.
➢ Students create a "family circle" or "community circle" for class discussion.
➢ Students' parents decide to have a class discussion regarding class rules.
➢ Administrators decide to have an open school discussion regarding class rules.
➢ Rules become part of class discussion regarding a just and fair system in a school.

What other types of classroom practices can you think of that demonstrate **Justice** and **Fairness** for this curriculum unit? After you have tried one of these practices, reflect on the elements of **LF**, **JF**, and **EEO**.

Applied Project

Reflect on themes of **Justice and Fairness** in democratic practice and create a scenario in response to the case at Mountain High School or a case study of your own. Think about the elements of **JF** in the case about career day. What other events have you observed?

Compare your response with that of another student. Peer review and reflect.

Strength of his/her answer:

Strength of your answer:

A Case Study

Equality and Equal Opportunity

Concept for Application: Thomas Paine—Individual's ability to reason must be promoted. Social inventions constrain humanity.

Mountain Cactus Junior High School

The students at the junior high are writing narratives for a story contest. The award for the best story is a financial gift from several community groups for excellence in writing. While the students have had their overall topic approved by their classroom teacher, no one has expected that the students would choose to write about controversial topics such as violence and the use of drugs. Furthermore, some of the parents are insisting that the students who wrote about such topics be disqualified from competition. The parents of the students who wrote the essays feel that their students did not write to incite but, rather, to explore the topic, and this type of disqualification is a constraint on the individuality of a writer.

Reflection on Practice

Sample Extended Questions

- ➤ What would you say to each group of parents?
- ➤ What choices can an educator make to ensure that social inventions do not constrain man?
- ➤ What would you do differently?
- ➤ When should humans be constrained? Ever?
- ➤ What would you say to the students who wrote the report?

Notes

Students' Role in Questioning

Can a democracy provide for **Equality** and **Equal Opportunity** for all of its citizens?
Is inequality ever fair in a democracy?

Think about issues of **Equality** and **Equal Opportunity**

Answer the questions above and describe the role of the teacher in determining **E** and **EO** in student work.

Compare your answer with that of another student. What do you think of his/her answer?

Strengths of his/her answer

Strengths of your answer

Example Curriculum Project

> Think about issues of Equality and Equal Opportunity.

Individual in History: Paulo Freire
Literacy is a means of empowerment. All citizens should be well educated in order to create an awareness of oppression.

At River Elementary School, parents are concerned that some children prefer a non-graded project instead of graded projects. One parent spoke to the classroom teacher about not finding enough outside time to get to the library to help her student write a report. Another feels that not all children have access to technology and use of the Internet is not available. They feel that a non-graded report is justified. Thus, some students have computers at home, some have software to use (such as encyclopedias, net search, printers) and others have very little access to technology.

The activities below are designed to promote **Equality and Equal Opportunity in the Use of Technology and Access to Information:**

> ➢ Have students bring in files and file folders to coordinate their data collection.
> ➢ Have students who have home computers and software run searches for their team or group.
> ➢ Have students invite in family members and neighbors to tell about how they use computers.
> ➢ Have students invite local businesses to loan (laptop?) computers to the class for a short period of time so searches can be completed in the classroom.
> ➢ Teach students to use computers by taking a field trip to the public library. Ask the librarian to teach students to write the preliminary report from data they find at the library, including computer searches.
> ➢ Ask local colleges to send students preparing for technological careers to bring in their laptops for a day and show students how to use them.
> ➢ Ask the school to free up some of the site's library time for a student after-school or before-school search.
> ➢ Have students with experience in computers role-play with the other students so they become the teacher (students learn from hearing students' experience with computers).
> ➢ Have students decide on their own grade, or a rubric for their own grade.
> ➢ Create with the students the class-grading rubric.
> ➢ Be certain to use books and media found in public libraries as a model for accessing information.

> ➤ Assume the post-modern role of the *informationist* (see Appendix B) and work parallel to the students.

> What other activities can you add to this curriculum unit that will promote equality and equal opportunity?

Examples of Classroom Practice

> ➤ Students form study buddy pairs, or study groups of three to four students.
> ➤ Students bring in their own materials such as disks, video recorders and tapes, books, and maps.
> ➤ Students re-design the classroom environment, finding storage space as well as usable space or media and hard copy materials.
> ➤ Teachers work with students individually, in pairs or in their groups and guides, selects, and serves as a resource (and learner!) with the media and the students. The teacher's role is one of informationist (see Part Three).
> ➤ Students decide what type of technology and information is needed for their report, and how they want to use and share the available resources and review district guidelines with their teachers (such as guidelines for publishing work, guidelines for use of the Internet).
> ➤ Example formats for presenting reports could be any of the following: a videotape of report, the creation of a web site with ancillary information related to the report, a newsletter to parents with the basic information contained in the report, the use of e-mail to other schools to present their report and interact about topic.
> ➤ Teacher acts as an interpreter of information and helps students sift through vast amounts of information on the Internet, in texts, and in multimedia.
> ➤ Students determine how to best represent their work for evaluation.
> ➤ Students peer review the work of other students, both in their classroom, by media exchange, and in other parts of the world.
> ➤ Teacher co-creates (with students) the rubric for materials for final evaluation.
> ➤ Students create a classroom e-mail/chat area on the computer for discussion regarding classroom rules.
> ➤ Parents use technology to enter class discussions regarding class rules and class content taught.
> ➤ Administrator decides to have an open network of e-mail for all students and the community.
> ➤ Students can get feedback from teachers about grades or assignments on the Internet or a web page.
> ➤ Rules become part of a classroom discussion (on e-mail, in a web site) regarding what equal and what is equal opportunity in the use of technology.

What other type of classroom practices can you think of that demonstrate Equality and Equal Opportunity for this curriculum unit?

Applied Project

Reflect on themes of **Equality** and **Equal Opportunity** in democratic practice and create a scenario in response to this case.

Compare your response with that of another student. Peer review and reflect.

Strength of his/her answer:

Strength of your answer:

Chapter 4

Writing a Philosophy Statement of Democratic Educational Beliefs

A philosophy of education is a statement that reflects the educational and social experiences, (formal and informal) that have influenced your vision of what schools should do. **This vision or direction for schools is often called the goal of education.** A philosophy statement may also include a description of **how the stated goals will be accomplished**. This description of practice may be termed **the role of the teacher** *(or the type of orientation a teacher uses to his/her classroom practice).* For democratic schools, the philosophy statement is one that also encompasses the perspective of students (their visions, interests, and values). To this end, it is important that a teacher or potential teacher begin now to create a philosophy of education in a manner that supports the stated purposes of a democracy **(LF, JF, EEO).**

Several texts and series in philosophy of education may be helpful in beginning to write a philosophy statement (Feinberg and Soltis, 1992; Fenstermacher and Soltis, 1992; and Walker and Soltis, 1992; Oliva, 1992). A practical guide to writing a philosophy statement is found in the Stamm and Wactler (1997) text *Philosophy of Education Workbook: Writing a Statement of Beliefs and Practices.*

The Stamm and Wactler text presents four approaches or orientations to classroom practice. These approaches may be thought of as ways that motivate a teacher and represent his/her beliefs about schools and learning.

Review the four approaches to teaching on the following page and consider the basic tenets of each approach.

The role of the teacher as

The Executive
Teacher as manager
Student as consumer
Environment as task-oriented
Focus on the end product
Emphasis on the role of the teacher

Notes

The Humanist
Teacher as facilitator
Student as self-directed learner
Environment rich with multiple resources for students
Focus on self-actualization and exploration
Emphasis on the role of the learner

Notes

The Classicist
Teacher as expert and source of inspiration
Student as scholar/citizen
Environment appropriate to specific subject area content
Focus on specific subject area content
Emphasis on content and critique

Notes

The Informationist
Teacher as interpreter
Student as participant
Environment technologically centered
Focus on communications/community
Emphasis on the meaning of information

Notes

(Stamm and Wactler, 1997)

Writing a Statement of Practices and Beliefs

In writing the belief or philosophy statement, Stamm and Wactler (1997) suggest two methods to choose from.

The Chunking Method

➢ Write a list of practices and activities that you have observed at your school.
➢ Look back at your observation forms.
➢ Which of these practices and activities did you like best? Which did you like least?
➢ Find those activities and practices that you like best and identify an element of democracy (**LF, JF,** or **EEO**).
➢ Place the initials of that element next to the practice or activity.

Example: I like to use cooperative learning groups for hands-on activities with math manipulatives (LF).

Write your list on this form. Identify element(s) of democratic practice.

Belief Statement Method

Complete the following sentences in a narrative process of writing:

➢ I believe that the goal of education is . . . .
➢ I believe that the role of the teacher is . . . .
➢ I believe that students should . . . .
➢ I believe that parents . . . .

Combine your thoughts into a paragraph and be certain to use clear strategies for writing (active voice, present tense, a confident and firm tone).

After you have written your paragraph(s) that describe the role of the teacher, goal of education, and other such statements, identify each statement for elements of democratic practice. Review your observation forms for these elements (**LF, JF,** and **EEO**).

Example: I believe the role of the teacher is to prepare materials and lessons that will enable students to become high achievers. If they master the content of my course, they will be ready to participate in further education and in their choice of careers.

Write your belief statement on this form. Identify elements of democratic practice **(LF, JF, EEO).**

I believe . . . .

Chapter 5

Summary

The objective of this text was to provide a format for students in field experience to learn how to observe, identify, teach, and reflect on elements of democratic practice in schools.

Three main themes of democracy have been presented for reflecting on democratic practice and site-based observations. Forms using these three themes (Liberty and Freedom, Justice and Fairness, Equality and Equal Opportunity) have supported these observations. Qualitative tables have presented some of the individuals in history who have contributed to our understanding of democracy. Students have been encouraged to continually reflect on democratic practice through a review of these individuals and the elements of the themes of democracy.

Additionally, the values of character education and citizenship have been explored and the goals of the National Board of Professional Teaching Standards for Social Studies and History have been reviewed and used as a guide for observations.

Finally, students have used their observation forms to write a statement of beliefs, a philosophy of education statement.

However, the main objective of this text has been for all teachers, beginning teachers and experienced and mentoring teachers, to analyze those practices and activities that they implement and select every day and to become more precise in their classroom choices and knowledgeable about how to support democracy in practice. It is with this last effort in mind that all teachers, parents, and administrators of institutions of learning re-dedicate themselves and their efforts. Democracy is a learned set of values and a practiced condition (Ravitch, 1992), under which a society can benefit economically as well as politically (Dewey, 1933). Democratic societies provide for an environment of individual exploration and, thus, creativity (Dewey, 1910). While less the emphasis, Dewey also includes a premise that this creativity promotes national prosperity. Democracy, we could contend, is ever the open society of liberty and freedom and the body politic (Locke, 1690) where standards and values of equality must prevail for all. (Ravitch 1992)

Most outstanding to a democracy is its sense of justice and fairness. While struggling to support the individual, the individual's desires, and the needs of a larger group (the majority), democracy remains unique in history's governmental and social construct by virtue of its intentionality toward its most valued element—a just society. For a democracy to remain just, the fairness of its citizens' decisions must set it apart from any appearance of either the unjust or the evil of the world.

When deciding to build a democratic classroom, the teacher begins by asking, "Am I teaching fairness?" In so doing, a teacher aligns his/her practice with that of the true citizen of a society of goodness—a democracy that functions by the virtue and values of its people.

> For teachers everywhere, new teachers and those whose careers are well established, my hope is that you begin anew to analyze the circumstances under which you teach. Determine for yourself that your practice will be aligned with the goals for a democracy and that as you refine your practice, you also model a reflective practice that enlightens the next generation of citizens, our students!!

A Call for International Standards of Democratic Practice

Rationale

In an earlier work (Wactler, 1997b), this author wrote that the alignment of a teacher's role with goals for education creates a need to explore the social/political nature of American society. The inference of this exploration appears to be that teachers' decisions about their practices are based on their vision of society—that is, how they envision the construction of a democratic society. Teachers, Wactler wrote, are expected to define for themselves their interpretations of the elements of democratic classroom practice. If it is given that the United States has defined various visions of democracy, how can a teacher in training or a teacher with years of experience begin to address the question of what is Democratic practice? Furthermore, are teachers given opportunities to reflect on their own training? And, as Wactler (1997b) has posited, "Are those opportunities supported and promoted with independence of thought?"

When standards are proposed for any discipline, the effort appears to focus on those who would benefit from the establishment of the standards. For example, in writing about the goals of the standards written by the International Society of Technology in Education, the standards commission states that its "primary goal is to enable stakeholders in Pre K-12 education to develop national standards for the educational uses of technology that will facilitate school improvement in the United States" (NETS, 1998, p. 3). The standards developed in this document were created as a guide for effective use of technology.

If the establishment of international standards of democratic practice are to be established, it is important to identify the stakeholders of these standards. Internationally, this call is for the education community worldwide to begin to examine the value of democracy to their society and to support a collective set of standards that would support these values.

The following call is a process for the international world community to develop and refine international standards in democratic practice.

Substantive Support and Process: An international standards commission should be established to accomplish the following items:

> ➤ A statement regarding the importance of democratic practice
> ➤ Standards development in multiple content areas
> ➤ The standards development process—literature review, partnership, and stakeholder list
> ➤ Standards teams
> ➤ Feedback from content areas
> ➤ Working draft of international standards in democratic practice
> ➤ Stakeholder feedback
> ➤ Revised draft of the purposes and content of standards in democratic practice

A review of the educational environment that we create for students leaves educators and leaders wondering if we have a collective sense of democratic practice. For example, if we define our practice with notions about liberty and freedom, justice and fairness, and equality and equal opportunity, how can we promote a global sense of values in shared practice?

The following proposal addresses this need:

A worldwide set of *standards for democratic practice* should be developed to support schools in teaching the values of citizenship in a democracy.

A drafted set of international standards of democratic practice:

The following set of standards should be considered and revised by a committee of international educators, scholars, agencies, foundations, governments, communities, and parents. These standards are intended **as a call for action and review** that, while inherently incomplete, serve as a framework for future development.

They are however, a first call, a bell of liberty for the international community.

> ➤ *Teachers will become leaders* in teaching the values of democracy.
> ➤ *Schools will prepare students for citizenship* in a democratic society.
> ➤ Governments, communities, and private foundations will *recognize and support values* of democratic schools.
> ➤ *Parents will encourage* and support the practice of democracy.
> ➤ The *international community* of scholars, universities, business leaders, and heads of state will describe standards of citizenship in a democracy and *work with all people* and constituencies to *refine these standards.*

Educating Pre-service Teachers and the International Standards of Democratic Practice

---

In order to create a worldwide community of educators prepared to teach values of democracy in their classrooms, the following guidelines should be considered in teacher preparation programs:

> ➤ Pre-service teachers will have opportunities to *learn about the history and philosophy* of democratic practice.
> ➤ Pre-service teachers will have opportunities to *observe, define, and reflect* on democratic practice at school sites.
> ➤ Pre-service teachers will demonstrate *skill in designing lessons, practices, and activities* that teach the values of citizenship in a democracy.
> ➤ Pre-service teachers will be able to *evaluate their own democratic practice.*

Appendices

- **Appendix A**
  National Board for Professional Teaching Standards—
  Social Studies-History

- **Appendix B**
  Historical Roots and Definitions

- **Appendix C**
  Qualitative Tables

- **Appendix D**
  Curriculum Models

Appendix A

National Board for Professional Teaching Standards—Social Studies-History

Standards for Teaching Social Studies - History

The National Board for Professional Teaching Standards (NBPTS), a non-profit, non-partisan organization, supports the reform and commitment of American education (1997, p. 1). In so doing, it has embarked on a mission to establish "high and rigorous" standards for accomplished teaching. As part of its reform of national goals, it has created standards that help teachers reflect on their teaching and demonstrate their own growth and development. In order to receive a certificate of accomplishment in these standards of Social Studies—History, an accomplished teacher must demonstrate a high level of "knowledge, skills, dispositions, and commitments to practice." A Nationally Board Certified Teacher (NBCT) must demonstrate expertise in two dimensions: "the developmental level of the students and the subject or subjects being taught" (NBPTS, 1997 p. 4).

The Student Developmental Levels:
- Early childhood, ages 3-8
- Middle childhood, ages 7-12
- Early adolescence, ages 11-15
- Adolescence and young adulthood, ages 14-18+

For the content area of Social Studies—History, a standards committee of broadly representative professionals has created standards for assessment for the prospective candidate for NBCT. These standards are organized into three sub-areas: Preparing, Advancing, and Supporting Student Learning (p. 18). A review of the standards appears below:

Preparing for Student Learning
1. Knowledge of Students—Forming constructive relationships with students.
2. Valuing diversity—Encouraging students to value self and others.
3. Knowledge of subject matter—Using a broad knowledge of social studies and history to plan curriculum based on major concepts illuminated by history and social studies.

Advancing Student Learning
4. Advancing Disciplinary Knowledge and Understanding—Using strategies and techniques that engage students' interest and understanding of United States history, world history, economics, political science, and geography.
5. Promoting Social Understanding—Promoting the social aspects of the human condition, physical environment, cultural settings, and emerging trends for the future.

6. Developing Civic Competence—Developing knowledge, skills, and attitudes needed to be a responsible citizen of a constitutional democracy.

Supporting Student Learning

7. Instructional Resources—Selecting, adapting, and creating rich and varied resources for social studies and history.
8. Learning Environments—Creating and fostering dynamic learning environments (i.e., trust, equity, risk taking, independence, and collaboration).
9. Assessment—Using a variety of assessment methods to obtain useful information about students' learning and development.
10. Reflection—Using reflection on their own practice, on students' performance, and on developments in their field.
11. Family Partnerships—Demonstrating understanding and value of the role of parents and guardians.
12. Professional Contributions—Demonstrating regular work with colleagues, at school, and in their field.
13. (National Board for Professional Teaching Standards, 1997, p. 18)

All of these standards play an important role in the life of a teacher and the teacher's portrayal of democratic practice. Several standards are explicit in their support of the themes of **LF**, **JF**, and **EEO** (a discussion of these themes can be found on the previous page).

Of these standards, the following selective standards may serve as a focus for this workbook:

Standards for Emphasis in Observation

➢ Knowledge of Subject Matter
➢ Advancing Disciplinary Knowledge and Understanding
➢ Promoting Social Understanding
➢ Developing Civic Competence
➢ Reflection

Observation of the Standards of the National Board for Professional Teaching Standards—Social Studies—History Form

---

Focus on elements of LF, JF, and EEO.

Describe the Social Studies—History standards that you observe.

How does the teacher implement the standard(s)?

What is the observed behavior or reaction by student(s)?

What would you do in a similar manner to implement the standard(s)?

What would you do differently to implement the standard(s)?

Democratic Practice Reflection

Appendix B

Historical Roots and Definitions

> ## Liberty and Individual Freedom

How Do We Define Liberty and Individual Freedom?

We begin our definition of **liberty and freedom** (such as freedom to speak, freedom to make reasoned decisions) or freedom from (such as freedom from the oppression of the right to speak) by first reviewing two aspects of liberty in a democracy.

- ➤ Civic organization (the way government is organized)
- ➤ Social experience (personal values and experiences with the law)

When we review how government is organized, and then we review our vision of a fair and just society, we begin to describe what is considered our personal freedoms or our individual liberty. After we decide upon what constitutes our individual liberty, we then decide how we want to extend to our entire society these same freedoms or liberties that we want for ourselves. We call these social freedoms truths or societal values. In the case of a democratic society, the truths become the values of both the individual and the communal rights of the society as a whole. Finally, we hold these truths as "self-evident" (Ravitch, 1992, p. 38) and defend the premise for liberty and freedom—that is, we defend the right to critique governmental organization and the values held by the government.

John Locke, for example, wrote that it is through the consent of the citizens (the governed) that a government is empowered and that individual freedom is maintained by citizens as *they* determine the laws of their land (Ravitch, 1992). In an earlier description of Locke's emphasis on the individual as the maker of his/her own freedom and a free society, Wactler (1997) wrote that a democracy considers how government interacts with its citizens and creates laws of society. In a democracy, citizens create their own rule and laws and they determine how people should be treated. They **create** the values of society.

In the *Second Treatise of Civil Government*, Locke (1690) writes against the case of an absolute monarchy (Ravitch, 1992, p. 38). He states that, if people are born free, and civility is the set of truths by which a state or society continues this freedom, then any state that does support such "a perfect state of nature"(p. 38) exists only out of its absoluteness (as in monarchy) and not in the state of nature (p. 39). Clearly, Locke expected a participatory body politic where freedom to participate is valued by society, and then sanctioned by formal government.

Locke created a case for individual freedom by arguing that it is society itself that benefits when citizens are free. If one has a conscious sense of one's freedom, the body politic (the participatory citizens) freely determines the direction of the country and, in so doing, society becomes framed in civility. To become fully integrated in the process of participating in society and representing oneself in consciously thinking leads to the good of society and ensures the continuance of one's own freedom. After all, if an individual gives freely to society, he/she also can choose not to give to this same society. However, with full faith and training (education) of the full person, Locke postulates, social integration in the values of civility is likely to secure the rights and liberties of all citizens (Ravitch, 1992).

One example of the value of exercising one's freedom is the structure of a republic as a **representative democracy**. In the United States, individual citizens **vote for a representative** who will respond to their decisions (e.g., their vote). Voters also are free to recall the representative who does not represent their vote.

Justice and Fairness

How Do We Define Justice and Fairness?

In continuing a discussion of attributes of democracy, the definition of justice and fairness (as in what is fair dealing) surface. In the balance of thinking about what is fair, it is plausible that one would begin to explore notions such as what is fair and to whom. Thus, the fulcrum that balances decisions of fairness moves from a weight heavily focused on individual right to one that weighs more heavily for social concerns.

Two aspects of justice and fairness that should be considered in this discussion are

➤ Just conduct
➤ Fair dealing

Individual Right   Social Concern

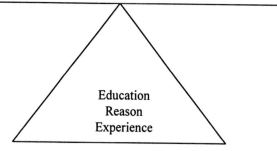

A review of fairness in governmental or social organization could begin with how one begins the process of reason. Wactler (1997b) reflects on Joel Spring's 1998 text *Wheels in the Head* and writes about a series of letters that defends both the freedom to reason and the ideas of learning. She wrote:

> *Spring's hypothesis (about justice and fairness) begins with a series of letters titled Cato's Letters, a discussion between John Trenchard and Thomas Gordon and published between 1720 and 1723. The letters were a series reprinted several times, in effect defending freedom of ideas and learning. Important to both the American Revolution and published on both sides of the Atlantic, the letters served to hypothesize that the link between freedom and civilization (society) is critical (1997b).*

Spring leaves us with the notion that, to be fair, one must determine the values of civilization. In other words, how do we develop the traits of civility (civics and civics education) to become a just and then wise society? Wactler continued to review Spring and found that his presentation of *Cato's Letters* idealized the link between freedom of ideas and prosperity, emphasizing most prominently that social happiness additionally supports the prosperity of humans themselves. Thus, we have a case for social concern with a potential outcome for individual happiness (1998). Further, to create a balance or fulcrum that neither eliminates free thought nor serves social needs exclusively, Spring proposes that critical theory grounds educators and education by allowing for free-thinking individuals who contribute to society's growth.

The alignment of an educated individual to fairness and justice is evidenced in his/her potential to make decisions that are both fair and just. The individual will develop skill in decision making, higher-order thinking, and questioning. He/she will not argue needlessly over the needs of either the individuals or society, since it serves human progress and individuals *both* when free thought and wise or reasoned thought will prevail. Wactler wrote:

> *For greater productivity, a nation requires the reserves of human progress, available only through the resources of free thought. The link then, between freedom of ideas and prosperity, is not only the obvious continuation of a state, conversely, the support of social happiness additionally supports the prosperity of man himself.* (1998)

> ➢ Is it fair to weigh for the individual?
> ➢ Is it fair to weigh for society?

Fairness may depend upon the issues, the society (as in school, district, or state), and the desired outcome of reasoned thought.

One example of the value of free thought in creating a just and fair society (in a democracy) is the structure of the methods of voting in a representative government. In the United States, citizens vote for a representative, but they also have access to a great deal of information to cast their votes. They hear the candidates debate issues. They seek out comments of fairness in reasoned responses. They ask that the candidates they select be fair and just, balancing a fulcrum that allows for individual needs and social concerns.

Equality and Equal Opportunity

How Do We Define Equality and Equal Opportunity?

Justice and fairness in a democracy give rise to a framework in which democracy clearly belongs: **equality and equal opportunity**. We ask in this discourse of a construct of democracy, is our social fabric, our social organization (as in organization for schooling), fair and just to all citizens?

An aligned response to the question of fairness is the question of equity. Under what circumstances do we define our schools as "societies" that are teaching in a manner that is equal and provides for equal opportunity for all children? If we reply that several types of equal opportunities exist, we should ask as well, "Are those opportunities to learn supported by teachers with both knowledge (content) and independence of thought (see also Wactler, 1997b)? If we respond that, yes, our classrooms are indeed places of equal opportunity for children, then what in our classroom practice can be identified and described as independent of inequality and supportive of the well-being of all students?

Let's review our goals.

In the foreword section of the text *Choosing Democracy: A Practical Guide to Multicultural Education*, Henry Trueba writes about the critical nature of education in realizing the American dream (Campbell, 1996). The most critical element of education, Trueba reports, is the ability to acquire "knowledge and skills [and thus]. . . . become empowered and a part of mainstream America" (p. v). He emphasizes that, as American teachers model and promote white mainstream culture, multiple other cultures often less familiar to the teacher are often excluded. They may exclude opportunity from minority students, devaluing their culture and marginalizing their opportunity for economic prosperity (p. vi).

In a discussion of equality and equal opportunity for a democracy, the voice and views of all of its citizens should be heard and addressed. Trueba argues that schools respond in a "clear, pragmatic and powerful statement guiding teachers, educators, and scholars to engage in substantive reflection about our educational philosophy, policies and practices" (p. vi). He encourages equality and equal opportunity in the American dream as citizens begin to analyze what is equal. Trueba writes:

> *We must start from what Freire (1993) has called the "ontological" need for hope, or the essential commitment to pursue human existence with dignity even in the worst of circumstances.*
>
> (1996, p. vi)

Trueba suggests a philosophical position of respect and appreciation of the language and culture of immigrants and action in the pursuit of human existence with dignity (p. vi). Further, to be equal, to partake of equal opportunity, American children of all backgrounds must be well taught.

Trueba refers to the work of Paulo Freire (1993) grounding democratic ideals in an action plan for democracy. Key to understanding Freire, Trueba writes, is "critical hope," often termed "critical pedagogy" (p. vii). Both terms reference the ontological (making sense of the world) and are inclusive of the skills (such as critical thinking, higher-order thinking, debate, and content knowledge) in which to do so. Trueba calls for "pragmatic school reform" and invokes the writing of McLaren (1989) who insists that for students to find equality and equal opportunity in a democracy they must have, as in liberty for all, representation, particularly representation in the scholarly world.

If students are made to feel that their culture, their language, their experience, and their voice are indeed "invisible to history" (p. viii) then the representation of that citizen may be invisible. To cast aside a citizen's representation may be the first step in defiling democracy. Contrast then, this crushing of equality with the vision of democracy, (as American democracy) by a foreigner, Alexis de Tocqueville. Tocqueville, an admirer of Thomas Jefferson as the creator of the American social condition, wrote:

> *No novelty in the United States struck me more vividly during my stay there than the equality of conditions. It was easy to see the immense influence of this basic fact on the whole course of society. It gives a particular turn to public opinion and a particular twist to the laws, new maxims to those who govern and particular habits to the governed.*
>
> (Tocqueville, 1838, p. 3)

Wactler (1997) wrote that Tocqueville truly admired American democracy for its consistency in social conditions, a goal encouraging to American teachers. She wrote of Tocqueville:

> Tocqueville, so enamored with American democracy wrote that it is the consistency of equality of social conditions that encourages the effect of creativity in America. The opportunity for this consistency marked for Tocqueville, a uniqueness of conditions and a habit of great admiration. To maintain this consistency, Tocqueville wrote a sincere tribute to America:

> *The mind became an element in success; knowledge became a tool of government and intellect a social force; educated men played a part in affairs of state.* (Tocqueville, 1838, p. 4)

Teachers, administrators, and districts are empowered but also commanded to review and revise curriculum and practices, to encourage and teach the skills of the intellect to all studen in a manner that is inclusive of social history. They should recognize the skills of all students It is of particular importance that the practitioner becomes familiar with skill in critical pedagogy (critique) as well as the skills of transmission of content. **Do these well!**

Appendix C

Qualitative Tables

Individuals in the History of Democracy

Consider the following individuals and their contributions to **Liberty and Freedom**

INDIVIDUAL	DATE	CONCEPTS
Thucydides Athens, Greece	440—400 B.C.	Power to govern belongs to all people. People are equal under the law. Wrote *The Peloponnesian War* as a metaphor for the values of democracy. The hero, Pericles, defends the rule of law and extends **freedom** to all people.
Plato Athens, Greece	428—347 B.C.	Individuals descend from self-interest to communal need. Result may be a shift in focus of democracy. Emphasis: **Individual Freedom.**
Aristotle Athens, Greece	1632—1704	Preference of Polity (democracy with elements of oligarchy and moderation); however, Athens introduced notions of **personal freedom,** rule of law, and importance of a large middle class. Emphasis: Numeric equality, majority rules. People are free when they can live as they like.
John Locke England	1632—1704	The consent of the governed as argument for **freedom** creates the case against a monarchy. A participatory body politic is necessary to continue a civil society. Faith (and opportunity) itself leads to free thinking.
John Stuart Mill England	1806—1873	**Political liberty** is so necessary that education should only be content bound (objective) education. The majority becomes the government. **Freedom of thought** and action lead to a steady improvement in the happiness of humankind.
Benjamin Franklin America	1706—1790	Independence (**freedom**) must be balanced by social needs. Without some form of government, despotic government (the end of freedom) could occur. Governments are not perfect but needed establishments, when well administered. Government **secures freedom.**
Thomas Jefferson America	1743—1826	**Liberty** is a natural human state. Given **freedom of thought,** each of his fellow human beings was thought of as capable of exercising powers as a citizen, intelligently and responsibly. A democratic state consists of a populace that is well educated.

(Wactler, 1998)

Individuals in the History of Democracy

Consider the following individuals and their contributions to **Justice and Fairness.**

INDIVIDUAL	DATE	CONCEPTS
Protagoras Athens, Greece	c. 490—420 B.C.	If properly taught, a human being can demonstrate *virtue and intelligence in the governing process.* He/she can learn what is right and lawful and what is good and that we benefit from fair dealing.
Alcuin England	735— 804	Part of the Carolingian Renaissance that encouraged schooling to children, including the children of serfs (workers), and improving knowledge through accuracy in language and books.
St. Thomas Aquinas Italy	c. 1224—1274	A scholastic and Aristotelian thinker of the Christian church. Justification of *faith and reason* giving hope to the use of intellect for every man.
John Locke England	1632—1704	Espoused a practical liberalism and the justification of popular government and argued for *consent of the governed* as argument for a just society. One gives one's freedom to benefit all of society. Social integration requires the training of the full person.
Jean-Jacques Rousseau Switzerland	1712—1778	Society potentially manipulates the weak. Personal freedom(s) can be lost to social needs and personal freedom would remain a priori to social needs. Inference to *just and fair society* and case against monarchy.
Maria Montessori Italy	1870—1952	First female physician in Italy. Defined potential success of mental effort that can be considered *just and fair* (e.g., that "mental deficiency was more an educational than a medical problem" [Smith, 1984])."
John Dewey America	1859—1952	Exploration or discovery supports democratic practice. Activism in thinking about one's teaching (as is reflection) is empowerment. Experience arbitrates and encourages the self to create knowledge. Society is maintained (as in a just and fair society) by the independence of participants.

(Wactler, 1998)

Individuals in the History of Democracy

Consider the following individuals and their contributions to **Equality and Equal Opportunity**

INDIVIDUAL	DATE	CONCEPTS
Cicero Rome, Italy	106—43 B.C.	Supported **equal distribution** of land (conquered) and rights for peasants. Wrote *On Oratory* as appeal for **wider and broader education** (than rhetoric only) in order to promote "wisdom, patriotism, courage, Aristotelian temperance, moral goodness, and oratorical eloquence" (Smith, 1984).
Benedict Rome, Italy	480—c. 543	Education should be (in his case, for monks) literate, **for the people. Children also** should learn **beyond the basics** of ABC's and be instructed in language, rhetoric, logic, and religion. Monasteries became an important economic and educational unit of their particular locality (Smith, 1984).
Mary Wollstonecraft England	1759—1797	Wrote *Vindication of the Rights of Woman,* an analysis of women's subservience. Proposed an **egalitarian alternative** to inequalities in British society. Proposed that pedagogy "served to empower or disenfranchise particular social groups." Espoused the ability to think rationally as a skill vital to success (Smith, 1984).
Thomas Paine America	1737—1809	An individual's **ability to reason** must be promoted. Social inventions derive from social constructs (constraining).
William Godwin America	1756—1836	Exercise of **human reason** rather than upholding a national agenda promotes human beings. Feared that society may engulf human beings.
John Stuart Mill America	1806—1873	The majority becomes the government. Political liberty is so necessary that education should only be **content bound** (objective education).
Paulo Freire Brazil	1921—1997	Wrote *Pedagogy of the Oppressed* (1970). Brought **education** to the **poor** and taught a dialectical method of learning. Created a consciousness for literacy as a means of empowerment. Interested adults in literacy for democracy.
Thomas Sowell America	Contemporary	Newspaper columnist. Promotes **excellence** in educational **attainment** as contributing to the strength of a nation, particularly the democratic endeavors of independence found in American government.
Amy Gutmann America	Contemporary	Education for democracy is essential. One's own ideas could result in repressive and discriminatory ideas. Lack of minority option is evidenced by lack of minority voice in social/political structure. All **curricula can impose** a value position and the human mind cannot be freed by objectification.

(Wactler, 1998)

Appendix D

Curriculum Models

The Tyler Model

The Tyler model consists of the following components:

> Student as source: Describe the student population.

> Society as source: Describe the demographics of the school community.

> Subject matter as source: The content areas to be taught are to be considered by their discipline needs. For example, if the discipline to be taught is science, is a lab setting needed? Will field work be required/are specific supplies needed?

> Philosophical screen: What is the school district mission statement? How does the teacher view the role of the teacher and the goal of education?

> Psychological screen: What information does the teacher have regarding learning theory, human growth, and development?

(Tyler, 1949)

The teacher considers these components in planning for a curriculum unit. The orientation to this development is largely a content-based curriculum, with consideration for the various sources and screens that enable implementation. Ralph Tyler's model was heavily used in the 1950's and remains popular for direct instruction models (Oliva, 1992).

This model aligns with the executive orientation to teaching (Stamm and Wactler, 1997).

The Taba Model

The Taba Model consists of the following components:

> Create a pilot unit.   Determine the students' abilities and align the abilities with curriculum goals and try out materials with students.

> Formulate objectives.   Describe the general goal of the objectives (similar to goals in this model).

> Select content.   What information and materials would you include for use in this unit?

> Organize content.   Describe the scope and sequence of the unit.

> Select learning experiences.   List the activities and practices of the unit.

(Taba, 1962)

This model aligns with the humanist orientation to teaching (Stamm and Wactler, 1997). The model is used in schools of progressive or holistic education. Constructs such as Seven Intelligences (Covey, 1989) are integrated into considerations of curriculum development.

The Oliva Model

The Oliva Model consists of the following components:

Needs of the students in general:	What do the students need to know? Refer to district and state standards.
Needs of society in general:	What are the values and social needs that influence curriculum development? Does the community workforce have an influence on the development of curriculum?
Philosophy and aims of education:	Describe the mission of the school and its vision for students. Who are the stakeholders or partners with the school? What are their beliefs about the role of the teacher and the goal of education?
Needs of the students of the school:	What do the students of this particular school need to know? Refer to district, state, and school standards.
Needs of the particular community:	What skills and abilities do graduates of the community schools need? How does this curriculum contribute to this need?
Needs of the subject matter:	Describe the specific subject matter resources.
Curriculum goals of the school:	Describe the particular curriculum goals for this school.
Curricular objectives of the school:	Describe the percentage of students who are expected to meet the curriculum goals.
Organize and implement the curriculum.	Describe the manner in which instruction will occur.
Specify instructional goals.	Describe the general skills that students will perform.
Specify instructional objectives.	Describe the specific level of skills a student will attain.
Select instructional strategies.	Select among the multiple strategies of instruction.
Select evaluation strategies.	Select among the multiple strategies of evaluation.

(Oliva, 1992)

About the Author

Caroline R. Pryor, Ed.D. (nee Caroline R. Wactler) holds degrees in anthropology as well as elementary, secondary, and adult education. She supervised students for the Office of Professional Field Experiences in the College of Education at Arizona State University. She taught mentors in the ASU Assessment of Supervision of Instruction course, the Beginning Educator Support Team program, and placed interns and students in four Phoenix-area school districts. She was a member of the research team at ASU's Professional Development School and taught courses in philosophy of education and curriculum and instruction. Her newly developed course, Developing Democratic Classroom Practice, is a first of its kind for teachers and will be taught at several school sites. Caroline teaches Philosophy and Curriculum for Northern Arizona University.

Caroline has received numerous awards for teaching and research, most recently receiving the prestigious award for Best Paper from the Arizona Educational Research Organization. She has recently authored the text *Philosophy of Education Workbook: Writing a Statement of Beliefs and Practices* (McGraw-Hill, 1997) and is currently writing an invited chapter for the Association of Teacher Educators' Commission on Democratic Practice. She is a member of the ATE Commission as well as the Arizona Department of Education's Commission on Standards in Adult Education.

1991. *National Council of Teachers of Mathematics. Professional Standards for Teaching Mathematics.* Reston, VA: The Council.

1996. *Core Values in the Classroom.* Tempe, AZ: Tempe Union High School District.

1997. *Social Studies—History Standards for National Board Certification in National Board for Professional Teaching Standards.* Washington, D.C.

1998. *National Educational Technology Standards.* Eugene, OR: International Society for Technology in Education.

Apple, M., and Beane, J. 1995. *Democratic Schools.* Alexandria, VA: Association for Supervision and Curriculum Development.

Ball, D. 1991. Implementing the professional standards for teaching mathematics: What's all this talk about discourse? *Arithmetic Teacher* 39, 3: 44-48.

Bennett, W. 1991. *The Book of Virtues.* New York: Simon and Schuster.

Bitter, G., and Pierson, M. 1999. *Using Technology in the Classroom.* Boston: Allyn and Bacon.

Bitter, G., and Pryor, B. 1996. Lessons learned for integrating technology into teacher education. *Journal of Computing in Teacher Education*, 12, no. 2:13-17.

Boyer E. 1993. In Morrison, G.S.

Burdis, B. 1987. In Morrison, G.S.

Campbell, D. 1996. *Choosing Democracy: A Practical Guide to Multicultural Education.* Columbus, OH: Merrill/Prentice Hall.

Covey, S. 1989. *The Seven Habits of Highly Effective People.* New York: Simon and Schuster.

Cranston, M. 1965. *Locke on Politics, Religion, and Education.* New York: Collier.

Crawford, J. 1989. *Bilingual Education: History, Politics, Theory, and Practice.* New Jersey: Crane Publishing.

Cruickshank, D. 1988. Profile of an effective teacher. *Kaleidoscope: Readings in Education*, edited by

Kevin Ryan and James Cooper. Boston: Houghton Mifflin Educators.

Dewey, J. 1910. *How We Think.* New York: D.C. Heath.

Dewey, J. 1933. *How We Think: A Restatement of the Relation of Reflective Thinking to the Educative Process.* Lexington, MA: D.C. Heath.

Doll W., Jr., W. 1993. *A Postmodern Perspective on Curriculum.* New York: Teacher's College Press.

Downs, H. 1975. *Heinrich Pestalozzi: Father of Modern Pedagogy.* New York: Twayne.

Eisner, E. W. 1982. *Cognition and Curriculum: A Basis for Deciding What to Teach.* New York: Longman.

Enz, B., Cook, S.J., and Omatani, B. 1998. *The Student Teaching Experience: A Developmental Approach.* Dubuque, IA: Kendall/Hunt.

Feinberg, W. and Soltis, J.F. 1992. *School and Society.* 3d ed. New York: Teachers College Press.

-------. 1998. *School and Society.* 4th ed. New York: Teachers College Press.

Fenstermacher, G., and Soltis, J.F. 1992. *Approaches to Teaching.* New York: Teacher's College Press.

Freire, P. 1970. *Pedagogy of the Oppressed*, translated by M.B. Ramos. New York: Seabury Press.

Gardner, H. 1993. *The Seven Intelligences: The Theory into Practice.* New York: Basic Books.

Glass, S., Kortman, S,. Lyons, R., Rutowski, K., Smith, G., and Spanias, P. 1998. *In Teacher's Toolbox: A Primer for New Professionals*, edited by B. Enz. Dubuque, Iowa: Kendall/Hunt.

Greene, M. 1988. *The Dialectic of Freedom.* New York: Teachers College Press.

Guttman, A., and Thompson, D. 1996. *Democracy and Disagreement.* Cambridge, MA: Belknap Press.

Havighurst, R.J. 1972. *Developmental Tasks and Education.* 3d ed. New York: Longman.

Hess, G., and Short, R. 1995. Evaluating communication skills of students in teacher education. *Educating*

Teachers for Leadership and Change. Mary John O'Hair and Sandra J. Odell. Thousand Oaks, CA: Corwin Press.

Hoover, R., and Kindsvatter, R. 1997. *Democratic Discipline*. Columbus, OH: Merrill/Prentice Hall.

Hunter, M. 1971. *Teach for Transfer*. El Segundo, CA: TIP Publications.

Jackson, P. 1996. Froebel and the hither jugend: The Britishing of Froebel. *Early Child Development and Care*. 117, no. 2:45-65.

Jefferson, T. 1944. *Basic Writings of Thomas Jefferson*, edited by Phillip S. Foner. New York: Willey.

Johnson, D.W., and Johnson, R.T. 1975-1994. *Learning Together and Alone*. Englewood Cliffs, NJ: Prentice-Hall.

Kohn, A. 1986. *No Contest: The Case Against Competition*. Boston: Houghton Mifflin.

Kyrene School District, Tempe, Arizona.

Lamprecht, S. 1928. *Locke Selections*. New York: Scribner.

Logsdon, B., Alleman, L., Clark, D., and Sakola, S.P., 1986. *Physical Education Teaching Units for Program Development Grades K-3*. Philadelphia: Lea & Febiger.

Loomis, L. Plato. 1942. *Five Great Dialogues*. New York: Gramercy Books.

Mill, John Stuart. 1977. *On Liberty. Collected Works of John Stuart Mill*, edited by J.M. Robson. Vol. 18. Toronto: University of Toronto Press.

Morrison, G.S. 1993. *Contemporary Curriculum K-8*. Boston: Allyn and Bacon.

Northern Arizona University Graduate Student, 1998.

Oliva, P. 1992. *Developing the Curriculum*. New York: Harper and Row.

Piaget, J. 1926. *The Language and Thought of the Child*. London: Trench Trubner.

Plano Unified School District, Plano, Texas.

Pryor, C. 1999. *A Model for Democratic Discourse: Curriculum Materials for Educational Foundations 670 Course*. Northern Arizona University. Reprinted in Democratic Practice Workbook:

Activities for the Field Experience. New York: McGraw-Hill.

Ravitch, D. 1984. *The Troubled Crusade: American Education 1945-1980*. New York: Harper and Row.

Ravitch, D., and Thernstrom, A. 1992. *The Democracy Reader: Classic and Modern Speeches, Essays, Poems, Declarations, and Documents of Freedom and Human Rights Worldwide*. New York: HarperPerennial.

Robson, J.M. 1977. *Collected Writings*, Vol. 19. Toronto: University of Toronto Press.

Rousseau, Jean-Jacques. 1962. *The Emile of Jean-Jacques Rousseau*, translated by William Boyd. New York: Bureau.

Schleifer, J. 1991. Misunderstanding the American founding. *Interpreting Tocqueville's Democracy in America*, edited by K. Masugi. Savage, Maryland: Rowman and Littlefield.

Schram, P. and Rosaen, C. 1996. Integrating the language arts and mathematics in teacher education. *Action in teacher education*. 18, no. 1:23-28.

Sharp, J. and Burton, G. 1998. Using a popular culture icon to help pre-service teachers explore mathematics education. *Action in Teacher Education*. 20, no. 2:49-55.

Slattery, P. 1995. *Curriculum Development in the Postmodern era*. New York: Garland.

Slavin, R. E. 1988. *Student Team Learning: An Overview and Practical Guide*. Washington, DC: National Education Association.

Slavin, R. 1990. *Cooperative Learning: Theory, Research and Practice*. Boston: Allyn and Bacon.

Smith, L.G. 1984. *Lives in Education*. Ames, IA: Educational Studies Press.

Spring, J. 1999. *Wheels in the Head*. 2d ed. New York: McGraw-Hill.

Stamm, J., and Wactler, C. 1997. *Philosophy of Education Workbook: Writing a Statement of Beliefs and Practices*. New York: McGraw-Hill.

Strike, K. 1989. *Liberal Justice and the Marxist Critique of Education*. New York: Routledge.

Taba, H. 1962. *Curriculum Development: Theory and Practice*. New York: Harcourt Brace Jovanovich.

Tocqueville, Alexis de. 1838. *Democracy in America*. New York: G. Dearborn & Co.

Tyler, R.W. 1949. *Basic Principles of Curriculum and Instruction*. Chicago: University of Chicago Press.

Vacc, N. 1993. Implementing the professional standards for teaching mathematics: Teaching and learning mathematics through classroom discussion. *Arithmetic Teacher* 41, 4:22, 25-27.

Vogel, P., and Seefeldt, T. 1988. *Program Design in Physical Education*. Dubuque, IA: Wm. C. Brown.

Wactler, C. 1990. *How student teachers make sense of teaching: The derivations of an individual's educational philosophy*. Unpublished doctoral dissertation: Arizona State University, Tempe.

Wactler, C. 1997a. *The Eruditio Project*. Arizona State University and US West Corporation Grant, 1997 - 1998. Tempe, Arizona.

Wactler, C. 1997b. *Post-baccalaureate students in early field experience: Alignment of theory with practice*. Paper presented at the annual meeting of the Association of Teacher Educators, Dallas.

Wactler, C. 1998. *Mentor teacher/student teacher response to European/American influence on democratic practice: A case study of a professional development school*. Best Paper Award, Arizona Educational Research Organization, presented at the annual meeting of the American Educational Research Association, San Diego.

Wactler, C. 1999. *When philosophy of education meets the information age: Student teachers' understanding of the role of the teacher in a postmodern world*. Paper presented at the annual meeting of the American Educational Research Association, Montreal, Canada.

Wactler, C., Stamm, J., Freeman, D., and Maldonado, C. 1996. *Teachers as partners in designing a teacher education program: A case study analysis*. Paper presented at the annual meeting of the American Educational Research Association, New York.

Wall, J. and Murray, R. 1990. *Children and Movement: Physical Education in the Elementary School*. Dubuque, IA: Wm. C. Brown.

Zeichner, K. 1983. Alternative paradigms of teacher education. *Journal of Teacher Education* 34, no. 3:329.

Zeichner, K., and Liston, R. 1987. Teaching student teachers to reflect. *The Harvard Educational Review* 57:23-48.

Zeichner, K., and Tabachnick, B.R. 1981. Are the effects of university teacher education "washed out" by school experience? *Journal of Teacher Education* 32, no. 3:2-6.

Zuchert, C. 1991. Political sociology versus speculative philosophy. *Interpreting Tocqueville's Democracy in America*, edited by K. Masugi. Savage, MD: Rowman & Littlefield.